To my son

TIMOTHY JAMES

born after his
father's death

Carol Sallee

Contents

Foreword

Jim Sallee was killed in a car accident on his way to morning classes at Hyles-Anderson College, where he was the head of the music department. It was hard to believe; Jim was needed by his family, by his school, and by his friends. He had so much to offer. He was an accomplished musician, a dedicated Christian, a consecrated soul-winner, and a faithful Sunday school teacher. His was one of those rare personalities that combined Christian grace and courage, scholarship and zeal.

Jim Sallee left behind him wonderful memories and a legacy of trained young people. His spiritual influence is still felt at the First Baptist Church of Hammond, Indiana, and his footprints are obvious at Hyles-Anderson College, where he served the Lord so faithfully.

Jim had just completed work toward his Master of Music degree at the University of Colorado. We are grateful for this, as we are for *A History of Evangelistic Hymnody*. This manuscript reflects Jim Sallee—the warmth of his heart and the height of his devotion. The book presents to us the thing he loved most—singing praises to the One he loved most, the Lord Jesus Christ.

Dr. Jack Hyles

Introduction

Men since the days of Moses and the children of Israel have expressed their religious experiences through song. Standing on the shores of the Red Sea, they sang of their deliverance from Pharaoh and the Egyptian army: "I will sing unto the Lord, for he hath triumphed gloriously: the horse and his rider hath he thrown into the sea (Exod. 15:1).

Every great religious movement has been accompanied by songs which, in a sense, have been a protest against authority, and against the long-established reputation and widely accepted norm of religious musical expression. Sects such as the Waldenses, the Hussites, and the Lollards each had their own hymnody. Martin Luther helped to stir up the religious fervor of the German people when he introduced "Ein Feste Burg" ("A Mighty Fortress Is Our God") into their congregational song literature. A century later Isaac Watts rebelled against the low state of psalmody in the established church (Church of England), led the evangelical movement, and later became known as the "father of English hymnody." The church was thrilled by the sermons of John Wesley, and the spirit of protest again asserted itself in the hymns of his brother, Charles.

The hymns of both Watts and Wesley expressed the individual's personal relationship with God. This was a great contrast to the objective expressions of hymnody of the highly organized and institutionalized religious sects. In America, the revival fires were stirred with the hellfire and Heaven-storming preaching of Jonathan Edwards and George Whitefield. The revival spirit demanded a more lively and enthusiastic type of song. This need was met by the folk hymns and spiritual songs of the frontier camp meetings.

Seventy-five years after the beginning of the camp meeting in 1800, the gospel song—the song of the urban revival—came into existence. In spite of criticism and negative predictions by writers on church music during the first part of the twentieth century, the gospel song is still at the forefront of evangelistic hymnody. And it is with the neglected subject of the history of the gospel song that this study deals.

Let us survey the history of what A. E. Baily has called a "distinctive American phenomenon," the gospel song tradition.

CHAPTER 1

Evangelistic Hymnody in the Eighteenth Century

Isaac Watts and the Subjectivity of Congregational Song

The gospel song is indeed an American phenomenon, but its beginnings must be traced to the mother country, England. There Isaac Watts (1674-1748) helped to bring a change from psalmody to hymnody. Watts' use of paraphrased versions of the Psalms and his freely composed hymns signified the beginning of a spirit of protest against the traditional psalmody found in the Church of England.

Until the time of Watts, the established church had sung rhymed, metrical translations of the Psalms. As a young man of twenty-one, Watts complained about the quality of these psalms. In reply, his father challenged him to write a better one if he could. He did, and presented to the congregation at the evening service a hymnic version of a psalm entitled "Behold the Glories of the Lamb." This was the beginning of a prolific career of hymn writing for Watts.

He sensed the need for a better type of verse to be used in the public service—a personal expression of the gospel. For, other than the hymnic efforts of Rev. John Patrick forty years earlier, the song texts of the Church of England and nonconformist (non-liturgical) groups had been couched in the expressions of Judaism. In his preference to *The Psalms of David Imitated* (London, 1719), Watts said that he had "brought down the royal author into the common affairs of the Christian life, and led the Psalmist of Israel into the Church of Christ without anything of the Jew about him."[1] With the introduction of this psalm book and its hymnic versions of the Psalms, a smooth transition was easily made between psalmody and hymnody, uniting as it did the Hebrew and the Christian conceptions.

However, the psalm paraphrases did not catch the attention of the public as did Watts' publication of *Hymns and Spiritual Songs,* published in 1707. Although these hymns of "human composure" were not the first of this type to be written, Watts had an unusual ability to express his ideas of worship in a poetic form. His view of a personal relationship with God is expressed in the hymn "When I Survey the Wondrous Cross," still found in gospel song collections today. The subjectivity of the lyrics is typical of gospel song texts. Note the personal expression of the gospel in these words:

> When I survey the wondrous cross
> On which the Prince of glory died,
> My richest gain I count but loss,
> And pour contempt on all my pride.[2]

There is good reason to refer to Watts as "the father of English hymnody." He almost singlehandedly transformed the psalm into the hymn, besides composing nearly 750 hymns of his own. One could also consider Watts "the father of the gospel song," because he brought a great deal of subjectivity and personal expression of the gospel to the hymn, the new form of church song. In essence, Watts set up new standards for the church song: (1) It should be evangelical, brought within the light of the gospel; (2) It should be freely composed rather than an exact translation of the Scripture; and (3) It should express the thoughts and feelings of the singers.[3]

The new movement of church hymnody begun by Watts, even though intended for liturgical purposes, was not immediately effective in influencing the Anglican tradition. His hymns had gradually replaced the metrical psalms in the nonconformist churches, but the remainder of the churches and chapels continued to sing the psalms. This was the state of congregational song when John and Charles Wesley came on the scene.

---

1. Henry Wilder Foote, *Three Centuries of American Hymnody,* p. 61.

2. Isaac Watts, "When I Survey the Wondrous Cross," from *Soul-Stirring Songs and Hymns,* John R. Rice and Joy Rice Martin, eds.

3. Louis F. Benson, *The English Hymn,* p. 110.

Revival Hymns of John and Charles Wesley: Melodic and Textual Freedom

John Wesley was born in 1703, and Charles was born in 1707–the year of the publication of Watt's *Hymns and Spiritual Songs.* The Wesleys were born into an Anglican home, and they both were ordained in the Anglican church. In October of 1735 they left England as missionaries to Georgia. While on board ship, they came under the influence of their fellow passengers, seventy-six German Moravian colonists. The Moravians were a devoutly religious people, and they sang much on the trip. Although the Wesleys were Anglican clergymen with a high church background, they were quite impressed with the Moravians' enthusiastic singing of hymns. This experience reinforced John's great dissatisfaction with the state of psalmody in the church, which he ridiculed as "the miserable, scandalous doggerel of Sternhold and Hopkins."[4]

The Wesleys' association with the Moravians during the trip and then in Georgia had an important influence on what was to become Wesleyan hymnody. Its immediate effect was to introduce to congregation; an enthusiastic type of hymn singing quite foreign to the sober singing of the metrical psalms. It also revealed the spiritual possibilities of the hymn. Eventually, this enthusiastic singing and the spontaneity of song would influence the music of the camp meeting.[5]

The Wesleys' first hymnbook was entitled *Collection of Psalms and Hymns,* and it was published in Charlestown in 1737. It contained seventy pieces by Watts and others, along with five translations by John Wesley. Although this first collection had little, if any, influence on evangelistic hymnody, it is significant that it contained no hymns suggesting the ritual of the high church. No provisions were made for festivals or sacraments, which is also characteristic of all evangelistic hymnbooks to the present day. This was a sign of rebellion against the authority of the established song of the Church of England.

In August, 1737, John was served with several charges by the Grand Jury at Savannah. Among these charges was an accusation that he had altered the church-sanctioned metrical psalm and had introduced hymns which were not approved by the proper authority. This event forced John to return to England the following winter. Once again under the influence of the London Moravians, John was converted on

---

4. Ibid., p. 222. (Sternhold and Hopkins compiled the widely-used *Sternhold and Hopkins Psalter.*).

5. Ibid., p. 224.

Wednesday, May 24, 1738. Charles, who had returned to England one year earlier, had been converted on Sunday, May 21, 1738.[6]

John and Charles then began a lifetime of preaching the gospel and of writing hymns. In the early days of the revival movement, both preached and wrote hymns. Eventually, the burden of preaching fell more heavily upon John, while Charles did most of the hymn writing. The message proclaimed by the Wesleys was that of an unlimited atonement and a free gospel. As they preached in the fields and wherever else they could, the message was to "all that pass by."[7] The urgency of the gospel which sounded forth in their preaching was reflected in their revival hymns. The texts were addressed to the sinner, and they also exhorted the saved to live for God. These two purposes of revival hymns—bringing the unsaved under the sound of the gospel and uplifting the saint—are still reflected in the gospel song today. In this sense, the Wesleys introduced the evangelistic hymn.

Charles Wesley was at the forefront of evangelistic hymn writing. His example was more or less followed throughout the evangelistic revival, even through the later revivals of the camp meeting movement. With his spiritual and literary modification of the English hymn, Wesley set a precedent: The congregation no longer expressed its thoughts as corporate praise, but the individual began to express his private spiritual thoughts and feelings within the context of the audible singing of the congregation.

Charles Wesley's hymns are also basically autobiographical. They portray in a simple and direct way his own spiritual history, which was similar to the experience of thousands of people of all times. In essence, his hymns relate the spiritual unrest of a convicted soul bound by sin, an instantaneous release through conversion, and the assurance of salvation. They also relate the Christian's trials and victories and his anticipation of a home in Heaven.[8]

The modern gospel song was foreshadowed not only by the words of Wesley's hymns but also by many of the melodies found in his collections. In 1746 he compiled *Hymns on the Great Festivals and Other Occasions.* This collection contained twenty-four tunes by John Lampe, whose melodies were greatly decorated with embellishments. Lampe, converted in one of John Wesley's meetings, was a German bassoon player and a composer of comic opera. The connection between his florid hymn melodies and his background in composing comic operas is

---

6. Ibid., p. 231.

7. Ibid., p. 228.

8. Ibid., p. 249.

easily seen.[9] One of Lampe's elaborate tunes, "Devonshire," from *Hymns on the Great Festivals and Other Occasions* appeared as follows in its original form:[10]

Harmonica Sacra, published in 1753 by Thomas Butts (a friend of the Wesleys) is another collection that included elaborate melodies. Although Charles Wesley did not approve of the overly decorated melodies, he recommended the book. But in 1761 he published his own *Sacred Melody,* an amended version of Butts' collection, with most of the more objectionable melodies omitted. However, some decorated tunes were found in even the 1765 edition of *Sacred Melody.* "Helmsley" is an example:[11]

---

9. Maurice Frost, ed., *Historical Companion to Hymns Ancient and Modern,* p. 98.

10. Ibid., p. 170.

11. Ibid., p. 157. (It is said Thomas Olivers adapted this tune, which he heard whistled in the street, to the hymn "Lo He comes with clouds disuniting.")

Note the dotted eighth- and sixteenth-note rhythm and the dotted quarter- and eighth-note rhythm which are characteristics of the modern gospel song.

The type of tune appearing in Wesley's collection was known for the repetition of words and for the breaking up of the lyrical lines. These melodies became known as "The Old Methodist Tunes."[12] The practice of decorating melodies was very common among the Methodists, who enjoyed folk music. It was, at least in part, prompted by dissatisfaction with singing psalms at an extremely slow tempo. The following hymn tune, "Bishopthorpe," as it appears in its simplest form (A) and in a version with melodic elaboration (B) as sung by the Methodists, illustrates this practice:[13]

A.

B.

_____

12. Benson, p. 240.

13. Christopher Dearnley, *English Church Music 1650-1750 In Royal Chapel, Cathedral and Parish Church*, p. 141.

The freedom of the melody and the text in the hymns of Watts and the Wesleys began a liberation of congregational church music. Charles Wesley's use of popular, folk-like melodies and of words that spoke from the heart in the language of the common man set a precedent for evangelistic music that has lasted to the present day. It is doubtful, however, that the Wesleys realized that their example would give rise to a melodic freedom far beyond what they themselves would have allowed.

The culmination of the Wesleys' work in evangelical hymnody is found in the *Collection* of 1780. This hymnbook summarized a new concept of the hymn: a subjective, personal religious experience expressed in a text and melody that the common man could understand. In the final analysis, however, it is not to this culminating work that one looks but rather to the new method of spreading the gospel—congregational hymn singing—which John Wesley introduced in Georgia. In the light of the new hymn's development, John Wesley's hymnbook, the *Charlestown Collection,* takes on new significance.

Augustus Toplady

Augustus Toplady (1740-1778) was the first hymnist of importance who wrote hymns for the evangelical movement within the Church of England. Although he was a strong Calvinist, Toplady included several of Charles Wesley's hymns in his *Psalms and Hymns for Public and Private Worship.* [14] Toplady deserves mention because his "Rock of Ages" is often thought of as a gospel song. ("Rock of Ages," however, does not follow the strict definition of the gospel song.)[15] As in the hymns of Wesley, the subjectivity of Christian experience in Toplady's hymns found its culmination in the gospel song.

Olney Hymns, a Revival Hymnbook

In 1799, three years after Toplady's hymnbook, a collection of hymns appeared entitled *The Olney Hymns.* It contained 280 hymns by John Newton (1725-1807) and 68 by William Cowper (1731-1800). The collection was named after Olney, the English town in which Newton and Cowper lived. This hymnbook set the stage for the gospel song.

Both Newton and Cowper had experienced dynamic spiritual conversions following times of extreme mental and spiritual testing. Newton, a

---

14. Charles S. Phillips, *Hymnody Past and Present,* p. 187.

15. For a discussion of the definition of gospel song, see Appendix.

rough, crude slave trader and sailor was returning home from Africa during a fierce storm when he became quite disturbed reading *The Imitation of Christ* by Thomas à Kempis. On that stormy night, March 10, 1748, Newton accepted Jesus Christ as his Lord and Savior.

Before Cowper trusted Christ as his Savior he was in bad health, suffered periods of melancholia, and was committed to a mental hospital at St. Albans. There Cowper experienced salvation while reading the Book of Romans. It was not religion that had caused his occasional mental instability; to the contrary, it was his faith in Christ which gave him the inner peace and happiness he knew.[16]

The hymns of Newton and Cowper, like those of Wesley, are essentially autobiographical, and they express the emotions of their composers' spiritual experiences. Many gospel songbooks today include such "Olney" hymns as "There Is a Fountain Filled with Blood," "Safely Through Another Week," and "Amazing Grace."

Olney Hymns is a revival hymnbook. It became almost as popular as the gospel songbooks of Moody and Sankey one hundred years later. Many hymnbook compilers then used Newton's and Cowper's hymns which expressed man's sinful nature and need of salvation. These hymnals containing some of the "Olney" hymns became quite popular in many denominations, thus helping to spread the spirit of revival. They became especially popular among the Baptists, who in later years had a great influence on the gospel song.[17] These autobiographical *Olney Hymns* became an important life-line of evangelical hymnody which eventually led to the gospel song of the late nineteenth century.

---

16. Phillips, p. 89.

17. Frost, p. 83.

CHAPTER 2

American Departures from Psalmody

Deterioration of Psalmody

The religious development of colonial America closely paralleled that of the mother country. Once again, there was a gradual transition from psalmody to hymnody. And once again, the transition was a reaction against the long-established tradition and widely accepted norm of religious expression found in the Church of England.

In the beginning, American sacred music was based on the practice of singing metrical psalms. The Pilgrim fathers brought to Plymouth in 1620 the *Ainsworth Psalter,* the first rival to the *Sternhold and Hopkins Psalter.* In it was printed each psalm with its new prose translation alongside, and a tune in metrical form. The Puritans of the northern colonies and the settlers of the southern colonies brought the "Old Version" *(Sternhold and Hopkins)* of the Psalms with them to the New World. However, other incoming settlers brought psalters such as the *Tate and Brady Psalter* ("New Version") and the *Scottish Psalter.*

The spirit of independence asserted itself in a demand for a new version of the Psalms, a version that would be closer to the original. A committee of New England clergymen was appointed to prepare a new psalter, which resulted in the *Bay Psalm Book,* issued in 1640. It was the first American psalter and the first book of any kind to be printed in the new country. The original included no written music, and by the ninth edition only thirteen melodies (which fit the meter of all 150 psalms) had been added. In contrast to 150 psalms thirteen tunes is a very small number. Perhaps this was one of the first indications that the quality of psalm-singing and congregational song in general was deteriorating in America, as it was in England.[1]

By the eighteenth century, ministers were protesting the poor state of singing in the church. One young minister, Thomas Walter (1696-1725), complained in 1721 that "the tunes are now miserably tortured, and twisted, and quavered . . . into an horrid Medly of confused and disorderly Noises."[2]

The decline of congregational singing to the level described by Walter may be attributed to two main factors—one cultural and the other musical. Henry W. Foote points out that the primary cause was the difficult conditions that existed in those times.[3] The hardships of pioneering in a formidable and alien terrain contributed to the problem. The settlers lived in small, isolated communities and were kept busy clearing the forest, preparing stony ground for cultivation, and building houses and roads. There was little remaining time for cultural pursuits. After the first generation of emigrants had died, the cultural values began to disappear. The memory of the music which the Pilgrims brought with them began to fade, leaving a vacuum that demanded to be filled with a different type of song.

Congregational singing began to decline musically as a result of several practices of psalm-singing used in the services. First of all, many singers paid little attention to the rhythm. In fact, American congregations did not use notes at all, for fear that such "formality" would make them look like Papists. Besides, few could read music even if they wanted to.

The singing was quite slow and became monotonous; lively music was thought to belong to the devil. The main reason for the extremely slow singing, however, was the practice of "lining-out" or "deaconing" the psalms. Since very few copies of the psalter were available and many of the people could not read, a deacon would read a line or two of a psalm, and then the congregation would sing it. Sometimes it would take as long as thirty minutes to sing a psalm. It was the deacon's job to give the pitch and to keep the congregation in tune. Unfortunately, many deacons were not able to do this well, which added to the deterioration of congregational singing. All of this, in addition to the fact that congregations generally sang their psalms in a folk style

---

1. H. Wiley Hitchcock, *Music in the United States: A Historical Introduction*, p. 5.

2. Ibid.

3. Foote, p. 91

(with many departures from the printed music), led to a reform movement in the early eighteenth century. This movement was first known as "the new way" or "regular singing" and later was referred to as the "singing school."

At this point let us trace the parallel histories of the singing school and a widespread religious revival known as "The Great Awakening." The singing school was a reaction against the musical state of affairs in the churches. Similarly, the folk hymnody of the Great Awakening expressed a rebellion against the religious state of affairs. Both movements were important musical and theological factors in the developing history of evangelistic song, which culminated nearly two centuries later in the gospel song.

The Singing School Movement

The singing school movement was originally an attempt by several young Puritan ministers to reestablish a more nearly correct type of psalm-singing in the churches. As has been noted, the poor state of psalm-singing had come about partly as a result of the oral transmission of tunes. Leonard Ellinwood states, "Congregations of 1720 were able to sing far fewer tunes than those of 1620."[4]

The first attempt at reformation was made by Rev. John Tufts (1689-1750). In about 1712, he published a pamphlet explaining the rudiments of music and a notational system which he had devised. He also included several English psalm tunes. The third edition of this pamphlet was published in 1721 under the title *An Introduction to the Singing of Psalm-Tunes;*[5] it was the first American music textbook. After this first attempt to improve the church music situation, sermons and other books encouraged a return to "regular" singing—singing by note instead of by rote. Also in 1721 *The Grounds and Rules of Music* was published by Rev. Thomas Walter who, like Tufts, was a Harvard graduate. This instruction book contained psalm tunes and an explanation of how to read music. These two "tunebooks" by Tufts and Walter marked the beginning of the very important singing school movement.[6]

Thomas Symmes (1677-1725), also a Harvard-trained minister, summed up one of the original intentions of the singing school when he asked, "Has it not a tendency to divert young people, who are most proper to learn, from learning idle, foolish, yea pernicious songs and

---

4. Leonard Ellinwood, *The History of American Church Music*, p. 18.

5. Foote, p. 97.

6. Hitchcock, p. 7.

ballads, and banish all such trash from their minds? Experience proves this."[7] In spite of this noble goal, time changed the founding principles of the singing school. It began with the idea of teaching people music in order to improve psalm-singing, and this helped to spread singing in general throughout the community. But the singing school, therefore, became as much a secular, social affair as it did a religious one. In fact, sessions were as likely to be held in the local tavern as in the meeting house. In the colonial society, few distinctions were made between the religious and everyday life; according to Wiley Hitchcock, "the singing school was a popular meeting ground for both."[8]

The popularity of singing schools spread rapidly before the American Revolution: they were known in Charleston, South Carolina, by 1730, in New York by 1754, in Pennsylvania by 1757, and in Maryland by 1765. With the spread of this movement and its continual secularization, new melodies were constantly in demand. The old, familiar psalm tunes no longer met the needs of the singing master or his students, and the taste of the masses encouraged the trend toward more and more musical freedom.

This demand for new music dovetailed with the contemporaneous religious movement called the Great Awakening.

The Great Awakening

The religious scene before the American Revolution was characterized by denominational schisms and rivalries. English dissenters who came to America for religious freedom found (to their chagrin) that other dissenting groups were looking for a different type of religious expression.

The Great Awakening, a movement that reacted against traditional religious institutions, brought the splintered groups together. It began in 1734 at Northampton, Massachusetts, under the preaching of Jonathan Edwards (1703-1758). The evangelistic preaching of Edwards, an American Congregationalist, and of George Whitefield (1714-1770), an evangelist and theologian from England, stirred the revival fires. This revival spirit touched many congregations, especially the Baptists in Massachusetts, and thousands were converted.

In spite of the rise of singing schools, the "lining-out" of the psalms was still prevalent in these churches. Many people, however, were dissatisfied with church music, and there was a desire for a different type

---

7. Ibid.

8. Ibid., p. 8.

of congregational singing. The slow and straightforward singing of the psalms was not conducive to the revival spirit; the need was felt throughout New England for a more singable tune than the kind contained in the *Bay Psalm Book.*

Edwards had brought with him from England copies of Watts' *Hymns and Spiritual Songs* and the Wesleys' *Hymns and Sacred Poems.* Although he still personally favored the psalms, his people preferred to sing the hymns of Watts. Edwards thought that the zeal for singing which had been encouraged by the revival was good, and he approved of "abounding in singing" in and out of the meeting house. This prepared the way for Whitefield's use of Watts' *Psalms and Hymns.*

George Whitefield spread the revival of the Great Awakening in the colonies from 1739-1741. Whitefield had been influenced by John Wesley's evangelistic method of using hymns, and at first he made use of the metrical psalms. However, he soon turned to Watts' paraphrased hymns with their subjective expressions of the gospel. The kind of evangelistic preaching of Whitefield encouraged the singing of hymns; the spiritual fervor among the people demanded an evangelistic response that the metrical psalms did not provide. The hymns generated congregational participation, and Whitefield encouraged singing not only in the meeting house but also at social gatherings.

Watts' hymns, therefore, became the songs of the people; they could be heard on the streets as well as on the ferryboats.[9] (It is interesting to note that this same enthusiasm for singing hymns accompanied the Moody-Sankey Revivals of the late nineteenth century.) It can truly be said that Whitefield introduced "The Era of Watts" in American hymnody.[10]

Music of the Singing School

Under the influence of the Great Awakening and of its leaders Edwards and Whitefield, another type of revival song got its start. The American folk hymn (or "spiritual folk song," as it was called by the late George Pullen Jackson) consisted of a religious text set to a tune rooted in Anglo-Celtic folk music.

There is no written record of this type of folk tune (until the beginning of the nineteenth century only texts were printed) but we do know that the composed music of the singing school was closely aligned with the folk music style of the British Isles. The singing school records

---

9. Benson, p. 164.

10. Ibid., p. 316.

suggest the actual state of folk hymnody during the last half of the eighteenth century.[11]

With the ever-increasing secularization of the singing school, the way was made ready for a new type of religious music. In the 1770s, the itinerant singing masters began composing semi-folk music which was considered "crude" by the cultured and educated. The composers called themselves "tunesmiths"; they did not regard themselves as artists but rather as artisans.[12] Many of these Yankee tunesmiths (most of them lived and composed in Connecticut and central Massachusetts) were influenced by the folk songs heard around them. The Anglo-Celtic folk songs, brought by settlers from the British Isles, stimulated the artisans' imaginations, and characteristics of the folk-song melodies were used in their compositions.

William Billings (1764-1800) was the first composer whose music reflected the Anglo-Celtic folk-song style.[13] His music also evidenced its antecedents in English psalmody. This new idiom was officially introduced in 1770 at Boston with the publication of Billings' *The New England Psalm Singer: or, American Chorister,* engraved by Paul Revere.

Although Billings is recognized as the progenitor of this folk style, the tunesmiths who followed fully incorporated its characteristics. Upon examination one finds common features of the folk tunes which indicate their Anglo-Celtic background:

(1) The main melodic feature was the use of gapped scales, scales that skipped one or two tones (one gapped—six tone; two gapped—five-tone).[14] These seemed to appear more often in major modes than in minor. Missing tones in the pentatonic (five-tone) scale were often filled in with passing tones supplied either by oral tradition or by editing. The extra tones, in effect, would make the scale hexatonic or even heptatonic. Scales similar to the Dorian, Aeolian, and Ionian modes were the most common.

(2) These tunes were rhythmically more varied than were their counterparts in Europe. Irregular phrases would shift from a simple, flowing rhythm to an angular and powerful rhythm.

(3) The harmony in folk hymns, although clearly tonal, stood in contrast to coexistent "art" music because of its parallelism and use of

---

11. Irving Lowens, *Music and Musicians in Early America,* p. 139.

12. Hitchcock, p. 9.

13. Austin C. Lovelace, "Early Sacred Folk Music in America," *The Hymn,* 3 (January, 1952): p. 52.

14. George Pullen Jackson, *White Spirituals in the Southern Uplands,* p. 161.

pure fourths and fifths. Unconventional dissonances were often caused by the extreme linear style.

The compositions of Billings and the other tunesmiths who followed him were bound into books that measured approximately six inches by ten inches and opened lengthwise. There were a variety of compositional forms, including odes, anthems, set pieces, psalm tunes, hymn tunes, and fuguing tunes. The fuguing pieces were the most popular among New Englanders; Irving Lowens calls them the "hallmark of the idiom."[15] Fuguing tunes were composed in a simple two-part form and were only vaguely related to the European "fugue." The first section was a homophonic setting with a cadence after two or occasionally four phrases. Each voice then entered successively (somewhat in the manner of a fugue). This second section was repeated, and then all voices came together in a strong cadence at the end. The form was, therefore, ABB.

Religious Folk Music

As previously noted, the semi-folk style music of the singing school leads us to assume that religious folk music also existed. The immigrant colonists brought with them Old English, Scottish, and Scot-Irish ballads and folk tunes. There are some passing references to this music in the writings of the time, but the music itself was never notated. Only the illiterate backwoods people sang it, and the more cultured city folk and ministers considered it less than respectable. *They* certainly would not have written it down.

It is impossible to pinpoint the time that the folk element first entered American evangelistic music. Just as the young and rapidly expanding America seemed to be heading in many directions at once in the eighteenth century, so it was with American hymnody. The folk element was just one of several divergent trends in American church music. The folk hymn style was clearly seen in the composed music of the singing school, but other evidences of this idiom also need to be explored. This entire folk idiom was the immediate predecessor of camp meeting and revival hymns, and therefore was the direct forerunner of the gospel song. As Henry Wilder Foote states, "These may all be regarded as successive steps to meet the demand for a popular hymnody."[16] Once again, we can observe that evangelistic humnody, the popular hymnody of the masses from the time of Isaac Watts and

---

15. Irving Lowens, "Our Neglected Musical Heritage," *The Hymn,* 3 (April, 1952): p. 53.

16. Foote, p. 172.

appear to have been composed in the folk idiom by Holyoke himself. In spite of the fact that both collections contained folk texts and tunes, neither met with much success in New England. This was probably because the country congregations already knew the tunes from memory and saw no need to purchase the hymnal, and because the older members of the congregation considered the folk tunes "illegitimate." Ingalls and Holyoke were slightly ahead of the times, but as the revival movement took on the new setting of the camp meeting, at least thirty such books were compiled between 1810 and 1844.

During the first two decades of the nineteenth century, this American idiom of folk hymnody produced a new offshoot which became the hymnody of the evangelistic revival. The folk-like fuguing tune and psalm tune of the singing school joined forces with the folk hymn of the country congregations (of the Baptists in particular). Under the impetus of the Great Revival in the early 1800s, this new evangelistic hymnody appeared in printed form. While the urban singing schools declined in the North, the composed folk-like music and folk hymn migrated to the South and to the West. A new surge of immigrants carried this music from Philadelphia to Harrisburg, to Pittsburgh, to Virginia, and then to the territories of Kentucky, Tennessee, Missouri, and Ohio. The singing school became popular again, but this time in a rural setting. The composer-compilers retained some of the old music and composed new music in the old style. It was this music—spiritual folk songs and revival hymns—that became known in total as the "Southern folk hymnody tradition."[22] This tradition was an antecedent of the gospel song.

The Great Revival and Its Music

Before the American Revolution, America experienced a great revival movement fostered by Jonathan Edwards and George Whitefield. While America was growing rapidly with the great influx of immigrants from Europe, Edwards and Whitefield responded to the call to "preach the gospel to every creature" (Mark 16:15). The Great Revival of the early 1880s was also a response to heed the biblical command to evangelize. The social, political, and economic conditions before and after the American Revolution had set the stage for revival.

Although the Baptists and Methodists were making gains in evangelization, religious indifference was also widespread. W. T. Whitley

---

22. Lowens, "Our Neglected Musical Heritage," p. 54.

details two factors contributing to this indifference: the rise of deism and the economic slump.[23]

The English philosophy of deism was promoted in America by Thomas Jefferson, Benjamin Franklin, and Thomas Paine. Paine's *Age of Reason* (a copy of the book could be found in most every community by 1798) was at least partly responsible for the popularity of deism. The deistic philosophy of rationalism that posited a remote, impersonal God found favor among many people and eventually resulted in the forming of the Unitarian groups.

Secondly, because of an economic slump after the Revolutionary War, the population started moving westward. This steady migration west continued until the 1820s, when prosperity began to return. As people migrated, they had a tendency to lose some of their cultural values. Their lives and attitudes were changed by the rough and crude frontier life. Once again, they cleared the land, cultivated the fields, and lived in small isolated communities, as their parents had done along the Atlantic coast. These frontiersmen left many of their social and religious traditions behind as they expressed their distinct individualism in a pioneering spirit. These were the very people who found the Baptists' message of democracy and simple faith so appealing.

Although this second religious awakening, termed "The Great Revival," had its beginning in the colleges of the East, its most unusual phase was found in the camp meetings of the "West" (Kentucky and Tennessee). Outdoor religious meetings had been held during the Great Awakening, but the camp meeting of the Great Revival took on new dimensions. Rev. James McGready, a Presbyterian preacher, is generally given credit for instigating the camp meeting.

Rev. McGready was licensed to preach in 1788 by the Redstone Presbytery of western Pennsylvania. He immediately moved to North Carolina where he preached in and out of churches for twelve years, emphasizing the personal message of free salvation and speaking against the formality of church membership. Because of the indifference of the Carolina churches, McGready in 1798 moved into southwestern Kentucky's Logan County, reportedly one of the most sinful areas of the frontier. Here he pastored three congregations on the banks of the three principal rivers—the Muddy, the Gasper, and the Red. By the summer of 1799 a revival flame had been kindled in these churches, and many were under the conviction of sin. As McGready preached, many cov-

---

23. W. T. Whitley, *Congregational Hymn-Singing,* pp. 84-85.

ered their faces, weeping, falling to the ground, and calling out for mercy.[24]

Early in 1800 an even greater manifestation of the revival spirit was seen. McGready had begun to plan for an outdoor revival meeting to be held in July, and with the help of many volunteers, he cleared several acres of forest. The pine logs placed in front of a high "preachin' platform" served as pews. Except for the "mourner's bench," a large area remained clear in front of the platform.

Thousands of people came to the meeting. They had traveled as many as fifty miles, a three- to four-days' journey by wagon and up to a week by foot. The worshipers brought tents, bedding, and food, since the meeting lasted for several days. McGready was joined by several ministers who helped with the preaching: Will Hodges and John Rankin, Presbyterian preachers; the McGee brothers, John a Methodist preacher and William a Presbyterian; Barton Stone, from nearby Bourbon County; and William McKendree, who later became an outstanding Baptist educator. In spite of McGready's Presbyterian background, the camp meeting crossed denominational boundaries.

The Presbyterians, however, soon disagreed about the new method of evangelization. The disagreement eventually resulted in a split, out of which came the Cumberland Presbyterians (who favored the continuance of the camp meeting). The Baptists, as a whole, took little active part because of their theological orientation toward predestination. It was the Methodists who soon became the leaders of this movement and who continued to use the camp meeting as a "distinctive method of . . . evangelization and church growth in practically all parts of the country.[25] And it was this first camp meeting, organized by McGready, that sparked these men to carry mass evangelism to all parts of the country.

The format of the camp meetings consisted of preaching, praying, and singing, but socializing played no small part in the gatherings. The people lived relatively isolated lives and thus the camp meeting fulfilled the need for people to gather socially. First and foremost, however, was the spiritual fervor that emerged. An account of the first meeting at Gasper River relates the following events:

> The meeting started on Friday, continued during Saturday, and that evening nobody went to bed. Instead, the whole camp was swept by an outbreak of repentance and confession. First, people discussed quietly among themselves. Soon the earnest conversa-

---

24. Whitley, p. 85.

25. Benson, p. 294.

tion spread like a flame from group to group. The excitement and tension mounted. People began to cry out. Old men and women, little children, young folks, parents—all began to cry for mercy. Turning and twisting, wringing their hands, beating their breasts, they struggled to be released from sin and to experience new birth in Christ.

All night the ministers and and converted Christians rushed about the camp praying and exhorting. In the darkness of the night, broken by the flaming campfires and the smoking torches, strange shadows reached out from the surrounding forest—the probing fingers of the evil one trying desperately to clutch the sinners striving for release. Here and there a cry of victory broke through the moaning as a saint was born.

Nobody slept. On Sunday several ministers again mounted the rough platform and led the singing with great booming voices. Again the people fell to praying and preaching. Nobody wanted to cease praying, singing, exhorting, and listening. Even food was forgotten for the time.[26]

The emphasis of the preaching was on regeneration. The evangelists preached hellfire and damnation, warning the people about an eternity without Christ. In contrast to the Puritan forefathers who believed that salvation was by works and that it took years to obtain, the camp meeting evangelist preached that when one turned from sin to Christ, regeneration was immediate.[27] This made the revival meetings extremely happy occasions.

Next to the preaching, singing was the most important aspect of these meetings. It too had its own special characteristics. The singing was accompanied by foot tapping, body swaying, hand clapping, and head rolling. George Pullen Jackson suggested that there was no need to induce the people to sing; it was sometimes necessary to constrain people from singing.[28] (At times, several songs would be going at once.)

Just as the preaching emphasis was on one's personal faith, the people sang of their own experiences. In the early days of the camp meeting movement, an expression of this faith was found in the hymns of Watts and Wesley, as well as those of Cowper and Newton. These hymns were sung to the familiar folk hymn tunes that were popular a

26. Jerald C. Brauer, *Protestantism in America* (Philadelphia: The Westminster Press, 1953), pp. 108-109.

27. In general, the narrative cited above gives a good description of the camp meeting activities. However, it appears that the author of this account has misinterpreted, as have many writers on church music, the Bible doctrine of salvation by grace. This doctrine was at the forefront of the Great Revival, as it was with the Wesleyan Revival and the Great Awakening, and is the theme of present day meetings held by Billy Graham and Jack Van Impe.

28. Jackson, *White Spirituals in the Southern Uplands,* p. 7.

> *Response:* Oh, I'm bound for the land of Canaan,
> Hallelujah!

(2) The call and response type:

Call: Remember sinful youth, you must die!
Response: You must die!
Call: Remember sinful youth, you must die!
Response: You must die!
Call: Remember sinful youth, you hate the way of truth
And in your pleasures boast, you must die!
Response: You must die!
Call: And in your pleasures boast,
Response: You must die!

(3) The one-line refrain type:

Leader: Together let us sweetly live,
Response: I am bound for the land of Canaan;
Leader: Oh, Canaan is my happy home,
Response: I am bound for the land of Canaan. [34]

These texts show that the spiritual song was an important link between the subjective hymns of Watts, Wesley, Cowper, and Newton, and the modern gospel song. Louis Benson gives a vivid description of the text of the camp meeting hymn:

> It is individualistic, and deals with the rescue of a sinner: sometimes in direct appeal to "sinners," "backsliders," or "mourners;" sometimes by reciting the terms of salvation; sometimes as a narrative of personal experience for his warning or encouragement. The Camp-Meeting Hymn is not churchly, but the companionships of the rough journey of the camp reappear in songs of a common pilgrimage to Canaan, the meetings and partings on the ground typify the reunion of believers in Heaven, and the military suggestions of the encampment furnish many themes for songs of a militant host, brothers in arms in the battle of the Lord. . . . A longing for the heavenly rest and a vivid portrayal of the pains of hell were both characteristic; and a very special group of hymns was designed for the instruction and encouragement of the "seekers," who at the close of the sermon came forward to stand, or "altar," and occupied the "anxious" bench. [35]

It is not difficult to think of several gospel song titles that fit these descriptions of the spiritual song texts. For instance, gospel songs that are directed to the sinner and backslider are "Power in the Blood," "Ye

---

34. Ibid., pp. 87-88.

35. Benson, p. 293.

Must Be Born Again," and "Is Your All on the Altar?" Songs of salvation and personal testimony are "At Calvary" and "He Lifted Me." Examples of warfare songs are "Sound the Battle Cry" and "Faith Is the Victory." "When We All Get to Heaven," "When the Roll is Called Up Yonder," and "Sweet By and By" are songs that refer to Heaven. The last group of spiritual songs, to which Benson refers as being for the "seekers," is known as the "invitation" song in the gospel song tradition. Examples are "Almost Persuaded" and "Why Not Now?"

Orthodox hymns were also adapted to the camp meeting style, the original hymn made more usable by adding chorus and interpolating folk-like lyrics. For example, John Newton's "Amazing Grace" as transcribed by R. F. M. Mann:

> Amazing grace, how sweet the sound!
> That saved a wretch like me;
> I once was lost but now am found,
> Was blind but now I see.

> Shout, shout for glory,
> Shout, shout aloud for glory;
> Brother, sister, mourner,
> All shout glory hallelujah. [36]

Also note Charlotte Elliott's "Just As I Am" as transcribed by H. S. Rees:

> Just as I am, without one plea,
> O pity me, my Savior!
> Save that blood was shed for me,
> O pity me, my Savior!

> *Chorus*

> Is there any mercy here?
> O pity me, my Lord!
> And I'll sing halle hallelujah. [37]

Watts' "Alas, and did my Savior bleed" as transcribed by Leonard Breedlove:

> Alas, and did my Savior bleed
> And did my Sov'reign die.

> I have but one more river to cross
> And then I'll be at rest. [38]

---

36. Jackson, *White Spirituals in the Southern Uplands,* pp. 224-25.

37. Ibid., p. 228.

38. B. F. White and E. J. King, *The Sacred Harp,* p. 290.

A different version of this same hymn is transcribed by J. P. Rees:

> Alas, and did my Savior bleed
> And did my Sov'reign die?
> Would he devote that sacred head
> For such a worm as I?
>
> O who is like Jesus?
> Hallelujah, praise the Lord
> There's none like Jesus,
> Love and serve the Lord. [39]

This hymn appears in modern gospel song books under the title "At the Cross," by Ralph E. Hudson. Hudson also added a chorus and composed music for both the verse and the chorus. The lyrics of the chorus are:

> At the cross, at the cross
> where I first saw the light,
> And the burden of my heart rolled away,
> It was there by faith I received my sight,
> And now I am happy all the day! [40]

The camp meeting hymns followed the precedent set by Wesley of combining secular folk songs with religious words. The tunes of folk hymns developed during the Great Awakening made an easy transition into the religious environment of the camp meeting; little change took place in them. The most significant difference made in adapting secular folk tunes to the camp meeting hymns was that fewer personal liberties could be taken in the interpretation of the tune. For the most part, one version of the tune had to be agreed upon for group singing, although few became completely standardized.

The participants in the camp meetings left little recorded information describing the sound of the singing, but there are a few accounts given here and there. In the early days, there was no "song leader" as is known today; the preacher would start the song. Lucius Bellinger, a Southern revivalist, gave this account in his autobiography, *Stray Leaves from the Portfolio of a Local Methodist Preacher.* He wrote of a preacher who led the singing: "He was a man with a sharp, strong, piercing voice. We now have old-time singing—clear, loud, and ringing." [41]

---

39. Ibid., p. 375.

40. Ralph E. Hudson, "At the Cross," from *Living Hymns,* Alfred B. Smith, ed., p. 129.

41. Gilbert Chase, *America's Music,* p. 222.

Most accounts agree that the singing was indeed loud. Samuel E. Asbury, a descendant of America's first circuit-riding Methodist preacher, gives this account of singing in the old camp meeting as communicated to him by his grandparents:

There was no instrument, not even the tuning fork. . . . Some brass-lunged relative of mine pitched the tune. If he pitched it in the skies, no matter. The men singing the leading part with him were as brass-lunged as he. As for the women, they placed an octave over the men's leading part, singing around high C with perfect unconcern because they didn't realize their feat. The immediate din was tremendous; at a hundred yards it was beautiful; at a distance of half a mile it was magnificent."[42]

During the early days of the camp meeting, no tune books were available; if they had been, few could have read them. As late as 1837, William Caldwell referred to the tunes as the "unwritten music" of the Methodists, Baptists, and Presbyterians. If notation of these tunes had been left solely to the camp meeting people, they probably would not have been recorded at all.[43] One of the leaders of the time expressed his viewpoint in *Zion's Songster:* "By rule I never learned to sing, Artless my harmony I bring."[44]

The "Fasola" Tradition

At this point the "Fasola" tradition must be mentioned. The "Fasola" people got their name from their devotion to the fa-so-la-mi system brought over by the early colonists. The "Fasola" Singing School music was parallel to and interdependent with the camp meeting hymn. George Pullen Jackson suggests that the original motivation of the "Fasola" people may have been to strengthen the singing school institution and increase the market for their books.[45] In any event, they must be given credit for propagating the spirited song of the camp meeting during the nineteenth century.

Few songs, if any, were notated in the early days of the camp meeting movement. Only the texts were prepared by some of the itinerant preachers and compiled under such titles as *Hymns and Spiritual Songs/for the Praise of all Denominations/as Sung in Camp Meetings.*[46]

---

42. Irving L. Sablosky, *American Music,* p. 38.

43. Jackson, *White Spirituals in the Southern Uplands,* p. 237.

44. Ibid.

45. Ibid.

46. Chase, p. 186.

The country singing masters, however, soon began to compile the spiritual songs along with their singing manuals. The format of the new books was similar to those of Billings, Walter, and Tufts; but they differed in that they included previously unprinted folk hymn tunes. They also contained a new, simplified system of "shaped-notes" in the attached singing manuals. This new system was probably at least partly responsible for the continuation of the kind of popular religious music exemplified in the folk hymn tradition.

In the North, the singing school and its music, based on a folk idiom, was rapidly losing ground as the New England society became urbanized. However, the rural singing masters did not take up the "new-fangled notions and scientific innovations" of the urban culture. They preferred to retain the fa-so-la-mi solmization system, to which was added "shaped-notes," a scheme of different shaped characters for each syllable.

William Little and William Smith first introduced the "shaped-notes" system in *The Easy Instructor* (published in 1802, but copyrighted in 1798). Andrew Law claims the primacy for this system in his *Musical Primer* (1803), but research seems to bear out the fact that he borrowed it from *The Easy Instructor*. In Little's and Smith's system, the shapes of the notes differed according to their position in the scale. The syllables at that time were faw, sol, law, faw, sol, law, mi, faw instead of do, re, mi, fa, sol, la, ti, do; hence, only four shapes were needed to distinguish the syllables:[47]

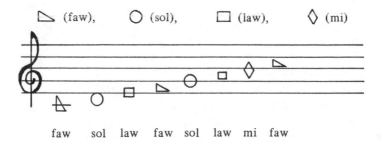

This system proved practical and many influential tune books in the following years were printed with shaped-notes. This same four-shaped-note system is still propagated today in the *Old Sacred Harp* tradition.

During the last half of the nineteenth century, a new, seven shaped-note scheme developed. Jesse B. Aikin in his *Christian Minstrel* (Philadelphia, 1846) introduced the system which, in essence, adapts seven

---

47. Dorothy D. Horn, *Sing to Me of Heaven*, p. 6.

shapes to the European system of solmization using seven syllables (do-re-mi-fa-sol-la-si). Other seven shaped-note systems were invented, but Aikin's became generally accepted. Basically, he added three more shapes to the four already in use:[48]

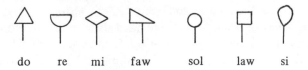

do   re   mi   faw   sol   law   si

This seven shaped-note system had far-reaching implications. Many gospel songs even today are printed in shaped notations.[49] The collections to be mentioned in the following discussion were, for the most part, printed with the four shapes. The notable exception was William Walker's *Christian Harmony,* which was printed in a seven shaped-note system of his own invention.

The first publications of revival songs were not primarily intended for use in revivals but rather in the promotion of singing schools. George Pullen Jackson credits Jeremiah Ingalls' *Christian Harmony* of 1805 as the first book published which contained spiritual songs; Irving Lowens, however, as previously mentioned, believed that Holyoke was the first to publish such a book. In any event, both were Northern collections, and they were far from the activity of the Southern camp meeting. It was not until 1816 that the Southern history of the printed spiritual folk song began.

Ananias Davisson (1780-1857), an elder of the Presbyterian Church, compiled 144 folk hymn tunes in a collection entitled *Kentucky Harmony* and had it published at Harrisonburg, Virginia, in 1816. Not only was this the *first* Southern collection, but it was the collection that song book compilers who followed used as a source; they patterned their collections after *Kentucky Harmony.* Davisson himself drew on the collections of singing masters who preceded him, such as Billings, Andrew Adgate, Smith, Little, and especially John Wyeth.

---

48. Jackson, *White Spirituals in the Southern Uplands,* p. 337.

49. I directed a large church choir at Landmark Baptist Temple in Cincinnati, Ohio, from 1969-1974. Many of the choir members were elderly people ranging in age from sixty to eighty years. As it was a volunteer choir with most of the members untrained in music (I thought), they had a difficult time reading music. Most of the songs were taught by rote. However, much to my surprise, when we sight-read a piece of music printed in shaped-notes, they read it immediately, and it sounded beautiful. Most of these people were educated in Kentucky and Tennessee.

John Wyeth (1770-1858) was a New Englander who settled in Harrisburg, Pennsylvania (on the main route to the South). His first collection was the *Repository of Sacred Music,* published in 1810. It contained many psalm tunes and fuguing tunes by composers such as Billings, Holyoke, Read, and Swan, and its immediate prototype appears to have been Little and Smith's *Easy Instructor.* Wyeth borrowed the idea of shaped-notes and used them in his collection. This notation was to become standard in the South and accepted by almost everyone. The second edition, *Repository of Sacred Music, Part Second*[50] (Harrisburg, 1813), greatly influenced Davisson's collection and later was a primary source for thirty other compilers.[51] It differed in content from the first edition, since it was meant to supply the musical needs of camp meetings in Pennsylvania. A large proportion of this collection contained folk hymns.

Many compilations in shaped-notes followed Wyeth's and Davisson's. Among the more successful were William Moore's *Columbian Harmony* (1825), James Carroll's *Virginia Harmony* (1831), *The Union Harmony* of William Caldwell, and John Jackson's *Knoxville Harmony* (1838). Of special interest and importance (especially to Baptists) was *The Southern Harmony* of William Walker and *The Sacred Harp* of B. F. White and E. J. King.

"Singing Billy" Walker (1809-1875), as he was nicknamed, compiled *The Southern Harmony,* first published at New Haven, Connecticut, in 1835. It was one of the most popular song collections of the nineteenth century, eventually going through seven editions (the last in 1854), and selling 600,000 copies. The popularity of Walker's collection was due to the fact that he combined many already popular hymns with tunes passed down by oral tradition—tunes the people had known for years. The title page of the *Southern Harmony* claimed that it contained nearly one hundred such tunes never before printed. In addition, these tunes were printed in the easy-to-read shaped notation. The music found in this and other Walker collections consisted of (1) anthems and fuguing tunes, (2) popular music, Mason School hymn tunes, Sunday school hymns, and gospel songs, and (3) religious folk music.

Religious folk music can be divided into three sub-groups: (a) religious ballads, (b) folk hymns, and (c) revival spiritual songs. As has been stated, the folk hymns of the last half of the eighteenth century combined with Anglo-Celtic folk tunes, and, through a process of

---

50. The *Repository, Part Second* includes the hymn, "Come, Thou Fount of Every Blessing" followed by the refrain "Hallelujah, Hallelujah, We are on our journey home." This is attributed to Wyeth.

51. Lowens, *Music and Musicians in Early America,* pp. 140-55.

simplification, produced the camp meeting's spiritual song. The nearly one hundred folk tunes that Walker harmonized are included among 550 folk melodies classified and identified by George Pullen Jackson in his *Spiritual Folk Songs* and *Down East Spirituals*. According to Jackson's classification, 550 tunes are divided into 111 religious ballads, 250 folk hymns, and 189 revival songs. He found that 347 of these 550 tunes have an organic tune relationship to secular melodies such as "Barbara Allen," "Cruel Mother," "Geordie," "Lord Randall," "Rejected Lover," and "Wife of Usher's Well." Even though these tunes originated in the British Isles, Walker and other composer-compilers added to them a primitive type of harmony which gave them a "distinctive American flavor."[52]

Within the several collections of sacred songs compiled by Walker can be seen one of the final stages of evangelistic music that produced the gospel song of the late nineteenth century. Walker's *Southern Harmony* reflects the heavy emphasis on folk hymns and spirituals which dominated the South, while his next to last collection, *Christian Harmony* (1866), reflects the reform movement of the North. *Christian Harmony* contained a large number of tunes regarded by the Northern reformers such as Lowell Mason, William Bradbury, and George Root (names often found in present-day gospel song collections) as more suitable for church use. The tunes of the reform movement (also known as the "better music" movement) and those of the camp meeting hymns are found side by side in *Christian Harmony*. Walker's last collection, *Fruits and Flowers,* clearly identifies the trend toward gospel hymnody. This collection for children is typical of the Sunday school songbooks of the latter nineteenth century.[53]

The Sacred Harp[54] (Georgia, 1844) was the last important collection of the "Fasola" Singing School tradition. It was compiled by a Missionary Baptist who was brother-in-law to Walker, B. F. White (1800-1879), and by E. J. King, about whom little is known. This collection, containing the same type of music as *Southern Harmony,* has had a far more lasting popularity than Walker's collection had. In fact, *The Sacred Harp* has had the longest continual history of any of the shaped-note singing books. It has been in use and in print from 1844 to the present day. It is interesting to note that this collection containing "Old Baptist Music," having gone through many editions,

---

52. Sablosky, p. 40.

53. For further discussion of the Northern reform movement and the Sunday school movement, see ch. 3.

54. B. F. White and E. J. King, *The Sacred Harp.*

was last published in 1968 by the Southern Baptist Convention's Broadman Press. Davis C. Woolley concludes the preface to this edition by stating, "It is sincerely hoped that this book may be the means of extending the musical influence of early Baptists of America as well as of creating a genuine appreciation for the musical heritage of Baptists."[55]

Although *The Sacred Harp* is an interesting study in itself, it is important to this survey because:

(1) Many of the songs contained in it are those that brought the camp meeting to an emotional and spiritual climax;

(2) It is a representative collection of folk tunes first used for religious purposes by Baptists during the Great Awakening and gradually put into use by other denominations after the American Revolution;

(3) It helped continue the tradition begun by Watts and Wesley of using popular music and subjective texts; and

(4) It contains tunes that have since been adapted to the traditional gospel song style and placed in modern gospel song collections.

---

55. Davis C. Woolley, Preface to *The Sacred Harp*, by B. F. White and E. J. King, p. iv.

CHAPTER 3

The Gospel Song: Culmination of Evangelistic Hymnody

The musical protests discussed so far against the staid, established religious music were all associated with the three massive revival movements since the time of Isaac Watts, the great hymnic reformer. In each case, the new congregational song met the spiritual, emotional, and musical needs of the masses. Such needs were expressed in a more popular type "hymn" which had two main characteristics: a subjective text (expressions of personal spiritual experiences) and a tune that was either of folk origin or composed in the folk idiom. Of this need for a lighter sort of church music, Louis Benson said:

> It thus invites, and, in the opinion of many earnest Christian workers, justifies a counter-movement to reach that element upon the place of their own taste and accomplishment. Hence, the Evangelistic Hymn, the Camp Meeting and Revival Song, and in our own day the Gospel Hymn.[1]

Henry W. Foote refers to the counter-movement by stating: "The Gospel songs represent a nineteenth-century phase of that search for an utterance, 'more to the popular liking' than the staid hymnody of the churches."[2]

So far we have traced the textual and musical antecedents of the gospel song up to and through the spiritual song of the camp meeting.

---

1. Benson, p. 483.

2. Foote, p. 264.

> Let all tongues of every nation Praise the Lord!
> For the gift of free salvation Praise the Lord!
> Joyful let our voices rise
> In the anthem of the skies;
> Let our loud exultant cries
> Now ascend to Heaven![25]

The tune is quite lively, with a swing, and the final word "Heaven" makes an upward jump of an octave.

The relationship between Foster's hymns and the gospel song can be seen in two familiar gospel songs, "He Leadeth Me! O Blessed Thought" and "Sowing the Seed in the Dawn-light Fair." The text of the former was set to what appears to be Foster's hymn, entitled "He Leadeth Me Beside Still Waters." Although there is some doubt about the authorship of "He Leadeth Me! O Blessed Thought," Foster's setting is very similar to the well-known setting found in most gospel song collections. The second song, "Sowing the Seed in the Dawn-light Fair," set to music by P. P. Bliss, is only a slight alteration in wording of the same hymn by Foster. This hymn became very popular in revival circles.

In most gospel song collections today, Foster's tune, "Old Black Joe," is found with the lyrics of "I Love Him." Without stretching one's imagination, a clear connection can be seen between the folk idiom of Foster's tunes and those of the gospel song. His tunes not only influenced the gospel song; they were actually adapted to gospel song texts.

The third person with a special place in the study of the gospel song is Mrs. Alexander van Alstyne, better known as Fanny Crosby. Fanny Crosby (1820-1915) lost her sight when she was only six weeks old. At the age of fifteen, she enrolled in the New York Institute for the Blind, where she received her education. In 1847 she became a teacher in the institute and taught English grammar, rhetoric, and Roman and American history.

George Root also taught at this institute. In the summer of 1852 and 1853, Fanny Crosby wrote the words to many of Root's popular secular songs, such as "Hazel Dell," "Music in the Air," "Never Forget the Dear Ones," and others. However, it is the writing of Sunday school songs and gospel songs for which she is best remembered.

Since she was four years younger than William Bradbury and the same age as George Root, Fanny Crosby was a contemporary of the

25. Charles L. Atkins, "The Hymns of Stephen Collins Foster," *The Hymn,* 12 (April, 1961): p. 53.

first writers of gospel songs. Her first Sunday school hymn was written for Bradbury in 1864, the first two lines of which are:

> We are going, we are going
> To a land beyond the tide.

This hymn was sung at Bradbury's funeral in January, 1868.[26]

From the beginning of her hymn writing career until her death, Fanny Crosby wrote over eight thousand hymns, hundreds of which were set to music by the most popular gospel song composers, including William Bradbury, George Root, W. H. Doane, Rev. Robert Lowry, Ira Sankey, J. R. Sweney, William Kirkpatrick, and Philip Phillips. She was under contract to furnish three hymns a week to Biglow and Main, publishers of many gospel song collections. Of the thousands of hymns she wrote (using over two hundred pen names) here are but a few: "Blessed Assurance," "Rescue the Perishing," "Pass Me Not, O Gentle Saviour," "Praise Him, Praise Him," "Saved by Grace," and "Jesus, Keep Me Near the Cross." In the introduction to her autobiography, *Fanny Crosby's Life Story,* Will Carleton wrote:

> All over this country, and, one might say, the world, Fanny Crosby's hymns are singing themselves into the hearts and souls of the people. They have been doing this for many years, and will continue to do so as long as civilization lasts. There are today used in religious meetings more of her inspired lines than of any other poet, living or dead.[27]

This statement is no less true today than when it was written in 1905. Not only was Fanny Crosby one of the great writers of evangelistic hymns, but her kind of "unquestioning faith in God's love and His Word" and "deep spirituality and abounding hope" permeated the writings of others who wrote evangelistic hymns.[28] Her gospel songs reflect the personal experiences of the Christian life as do the hymns of Watts, Wesley, Newton, and Cowper. Opening her eyes, she "saw Him face to face, and told the story—Saved by grace."[29] After forty-seven years of writing gospel songs, she passed away.

The long series of Sunday school songbooks (compiled by Bradbury, Root, Kirkpatrick, and others) demanded recognition for the part played by the popular type melodies in "developing a taste in the

---

26. Hall, p. 39.
27. Foote, p. 268.
28. Stebbins, p. 279.
29. Hall, p. 42.

young for the lighter type of religious song."[30] These Sunday school songbook collections prepared the way. As the work of the Sunday school movement mingled with that of the Young Men's Christian Association (Boston, 1851), the collections furnished evangelists with the first examples of gospel songs.

The Young Men's Christian Association

The Sunday school movement, and especially the Young Men's Christian Association, were the centers of the evangelistic movement and its hymnody until the time of the Moody-Sankey Revivals. The Y.M.C.A., organized in London in 1844, had as one of its objectives "the improvement of the spiritual condition of the young men engaged in the drapery and other trades." As the Association spread throughout the world its objectives broadened to include building "a new man and a new society, by a whole program of a whole Gospel, for the whole man, the whole country, and the whole world."[31]

During the Civil War, the Association did most of its work with the men on the battlefield, in camps, and in hospitals. It produced hymnbooks containing familiar hymns. After the war, the Association began a large-scale revival work in northern cities and supplied a hymnody more in line with revival efforts. Secretary L. P. Rowland compiled the first such hymnbook, *The Young Men's Christian Association Hymn and Tune Book,* at Boston in 1867. It was similar to the social hymnbook and contained popular hymn melodies by Bradbury and others. Dwight L. Moody, who at the time was the leader of the Chicago Association, compiled *The North-Western Hymn Book,* which included a larger proportion of the lively Sunday school songs of the Bradbury school.

With the ministry of Dwight L. Moody and his associate, Ira D. Sankey, evangelistic music received an official name, "the gospel hymn." This does not mean the gospel hymn did not exist before these men, but it was popularized and received its greatest impetus as an aid in mass evangelism at the Moody-Sankey revival meetings. The convergent efforts of many authors, composers, and compilers produced what Moody and Sankey called the gospel hymn. And the city revival, the Sunday school movement, and the Y.M.C.A. all provided outlets for these hymns.

---

30. Benson, p. 484.

31. Vergilius Ferm, *Encyclopedia of Religion,* p. 836.

CHAPTER 4

The Gospel Song: 1875-1975

The Era of Dwight L. Moody and Ira D. Sankey

In examining the gospel song as it is known today, one must look at it in the total context of revivalism. Since 1875 the gospel song has been the main musical literature of the revival movement started by Dwight L. Moody. This chapter will trace the final development of popular hymnody, exemplified by the gospel hymn,[1] as it has unfolded in the ministry of the local church and evangelistic efforts of Dwight L. Moody, Billy Sunday, Billy Graham, Jack Van Impe, and their associates.

The names of Moody and Sankey are inevitably associated with mass evangelism and the gospel hymn. Neither the message of Moody nor the use of a popular hymnody had changed from preceding centuries of revivalism; however, the different social and economic conditions which existed demanded a change in the nature of revivalism.

---

1. Authorities do not agree which term—"hymn" or "song"—is appropriate when referring to the popular religious song prefixed by the word "gospel." Moody and Sankey referred to their music as "gospel hymns." My preference is "gospel song." Thus, "hymn" will be used only when directly referring to the music associated with Moody and Sankey. For a discussion of the issue, see: W. Scott Westerman, "The Term 'Gospel Hymn,' " *The Hymn*, 9 (April, 1958): pp. 61-62.

In 1856, when Dwight Lyman Moody (1837-1899) was a young man of twenty, he moved from the East to Chicago. There he began his mission to reach the masses. His work for Christ began with a Sunday school class, but it was not long before he also became an active member of the Chicago Y.M.C.A. Moody had a burden to help the poor as well as those who were spiritually lost. He gave himself unreservedly to the work of helping the poor and also to the work of the Association and Sunday school. According to accounts of his life, he was a man of extreme sincerity and performed his work

> ... with all the enthusiasm of his intense nature, and ever with untiring energy, day or night; how he was the life and soul of every effort that was being made to reach the people with the Gospel.[2]

Moody had an abiding concern for the welfare and salvation of men.

During the last quarter of the nineteenth century, there was an unrest among the masses of urban society. Thousands of immigrants from Europe moved to the big cities and became a part of the large working class. These people had not been exposed to the spiritual awakening in the frontier revivals. On the other end of the spectrum were the "idle rich," many of whom were in big business and exploited the working class.

Many reformers tried to resolve this conflict. Moody believed that social renovation could only be effected by "the moral and spiritual regeneration of the individual."[3] He believed that when men were right with God, social reform would come naturally. It was therefore to this end, the salvation of the lost, that Moody worked. From 1870 until the end of his life, he tried to reach as many as possible through mass evangelistic efforts.

Moody's concern for man's spiritual and social condition changed the nature of revivalism. Early evangelists preached about the "God of Wrath and Judgment," but Moody preached about the "God of Love and Mercy." In the early part of the century, revivalism emphasized a journey to the "promised land" and the heavenly home, but Moody's emphasized the individual's relationship with the person of Christ. Charles Gabriel wrote:

> When all my labors and trials are o'er
> And I am safe on that beautiful shore,

---

2. Stebbins, p. 306.

3. James C. Downey, "Revivalism, The Gospel Songs and Social Reforms," *Journal of the Society for Ethnomusicology*, 9 (May, 1965): p. 116.

Just to be near the dear Lord I adore,
Will through the ages be glory for me.[4]

Fanny Crosby expressed this idea in these lines:

Through the gates to the city,
In a robe of spotless white,
He will lead me where no tears will ever fall;
In the glad song of ages
I shall mingle with delight
But I long to meet my Savior first of all.[5]

Revival movements had always focused on a personal relationship with God, but during the Moody revivals this was stressed to an even greater degree. Many Americans had moved from the highly individualized society of rural America to the urban society, each individual placing himself in a secondary group. James Downey refers to the insecurity and despondency caused by this change as "cultural shock."[6] Moody emphasized that there was someone who cared for the individual and encouraged him to seek Jesus Christ as a protector, friend, and brother. This idea is expressed in George Stebbins' gospel song with words by J. G. Small:

I've found a Friend, oh, such a Friend!
He loved me ere I knew Him;
He drew me with the cords of love,
And thus He bound me to Him.
And round my heart still closely twine
Those ties which naught can sever,
For I am His, and He is mine,
Forever and forever.[7]

Prior to 1870, Moody was holding evangelistic meetings for the Y.M.C.A. using this individualistic approach. His ministry was successful, but he was distressed by the poor quality of singing in his meetings. In 1870, however, Moody met Ira D. Sankey (1840-1908) at the Indianapolis Y.M.C.A. convention. Moody immediately perceived Sankey's potential when he heard a drowsy audience aroused to enthusiastic singing under his leadership. Moody told Sankey that he had been looking for him for eight years and, after much persuasion, Sankey joined with him.

---

4. Smith, p. 688.

5. Ibid., p. 697.

6. Downey, p. 115.

7. Rice, p. 234.

Although Moody was not a musical man, he had observed the power of singing in his Chicago Sunday school. He had used singing to draw people off the street and to keep their attention once they were in the meeting. Moody was interested in music that he could use as a tool in evangelism. Moody did not sing himself, but he said:

> I feel sure the great majority of people do like singing. It helps to build up an audience—even if you preach a dry sermon. If you have singing that reaches the heart, it will fill the church every time. There is more said in the Bible about praise and prayer, and music and song have not only accompanied all Scripture revivals, but are essential in deepening spiritual life. Singing does at least as much as preaching to impress the word of God upon people's minds. Ever since God first called me, the importance of praise expressed in song has grown upon me.[8]

Moody thought that a song which did not result in a response from the audience was not good music. He recognized that music for revival campaigns in the big cities and the well-established churches needed to be different from the camp meeting song that was used in a "free-wheeling" atmosphere. A change in the culture demanded new methods of evangelism. Therefore, Moody needed an individual who could touch people's hearts with his solo voice, as well as compose special songs if needed. Moody saw both of these attributes in Ira Sankey and gave the New Testament command to Sankey to "Come, follow me." The forming of this evangelistic team gave popular sacred song (gospel songs in particular) its greatest impetus.

In 1873 Moody and Sankey sailed to England, where they held the first of many successful meetings. Several writers on church music have mentioned that England was not prepared for Sankey's gospel hymns or his methods. Louis Benson, however, states that this may have been true of people in the staid and conventional churches, but it was not true of the masses whom Moody and Sankey tried to reach.[9] The way had been prepared for Moody and Sankey. Evangelist Richard Weaver had introduced solo singing in his meetings and had published several revival hymnbooks, the first being *The Revival Hymn Book* (1858). William Booth, the founder of the Salvation Army, began holding tent meetings in England in 1865. In the late sixties, Booth published *The Christian Mission Hymn Book,* which was followed by *The Salvation Soldier's Hymn Book.* These books contained many gospel songs and American Sunday school songs. Philip Phillips had just completed his

---

8. Hall, pp. 198-99.

9. Benson, p. 485.

second British campaign before Moody and Sankey's arrival. Phillips was a singing evangelist and his method of "singing the gospel" was widely familiar. He had also compiled a gospel songbook, *The American Sacred Songster,* published by the British Sunday School Union, which had sold well over one million copies. Thus, the Moody-Sankey methods were not a surprise to England.

The hymns and tunes of the British churches and chapels were not suited to Moody's evangelistic meetings. Therefore, Moody and Sankey adopted Phillips' *Hallowed Songs,* along with several songs Sankey had brought with him from his private collection. These unpublished songs immediately became popular, and many people urged Sankey to publish them. He wrote the publishers of *Hallowed Songs* for permission to publish an edition of that book with his songs included. When permission was denied, Sankey had twenty-three of these songs published in a sixteen-page pamphlet entitled, *Sacred Songs and Solos.* It appeared in 1873, just 166 years after Watts had published his *Hymns and Spiritual Songs.* This little pamphlet became the nucleus for the *Moody and Sankey Hymn Book.* Although it has been pointed out that the gospel song was actually in existence prior to 1873, some writers attribute its birth to this pamphlet.[10]

Gospel songs were relatively new to England, and in Scotland, where the team next went, they were non-existent. Only the Psalms of David were used. The hymns Sankey introduced, with their lilting, rhythmic melodies and ballad-like lyrics, were in extreme contrast to the grave and solemn psalmody the people were used to. Sankey first used the gospel hymn in a meeting in Edinburgh on November 23, 1873. In his autobiography, he related the following story:

> Much had been said and written in Scotland against the use of "human hymns" in public worship, and even more had been uttered against the employment of the "kist o' whistles," the term by which they designated the small cabinet organ I employed as an accompaniment to my voice.
> ... The service having been thus opened in regular order, we now faced the problem of "singing the gospel." ... The song selected for my first solo was "Jesus of Nazareth passeth by."
> ... After a powerful address by Dr. Wilson, and a closing prayer, I was requested to sing another solo. Selecting "Hold the Fort," then comparatively new in Edinburgh, the audience was requested to join in singing the chorus ... which they did with such heartiness and such power that I was further convinced that gospel songs would prove as useful and acceptable to the masses

10. David R. Breed, *The History and Use of Hymns and Hymn-Tunes,* p. 331.

in Edinburgh as they had in the cities of York and Newcastle in England.[11]

Upon examining the text of "Hold the Fort," one can see the appeal it had with its vivid imagery and militant tone and yet simple poetic content:

> Ho, my comrades! see the signal
> Waving in the sky!
> Reinforcements now appearing,
> Victory is nigh.
>
> *Chorus:*
>
> "Hold the fort, for I am coming,"
> Jesus signals still;
> Wave the answer back to heaven,
> "By Thy grace we will."
>
> See the mighty host advancing,
> Satan leading on;
> Mighty men around us falling,
> Courage almost gone!
>
> See the glorious banner waving!
> Hear the trumpet blow!
> In our Leader's name we triumph
> Over every foe.
>
> Fierce and long the battle rages,
> But our help is near;
> Onward comes our great Commander,
> Cheer, my comrades, cheer.[12]

This particular song also illustrates the fact that the gospel song was not designed for the staid "worship" service. As David Appleby states, "It was forged quickly in the heat of battle for the souls of men, and designed to produce an immediate evangelistic decision."[13]

That this type of song was successful in reaching its objective in Scotland and throughout the British Isles is a matter of historical record. Its success, however, must not be attributed only to its immediate emotional appeal but also to the methods Sankey used to present it. He was able to hold his audience—no matter the size—spellbound with his magnetic personality. Before he would sit down at

---

11. Ira D. Sankey, *My Life and Story of the Gospel Hymns*, pp. 56-7.

12. Philip P. Bliss, "Hold the Fort," from *Sacred Songs and Solos*.

13. Appleby, p. 145.

his small, reed, Esty organ to accompany himself, he would pray for God to bless his singing and use it to bring salvation to many lost souls. His prayer would often help to dispel antagonism, even in Scotland where people were not accustomed to either solos or organs in a public service.[14]

Sankey also emphasized the importance of understanding the words of the songs. But perhaps the thing which contributed most to his success was his sincere dedication and desire to see the lost won to Christ.[15] Sankey's success in Edinburgh and throughout the British Isles was unprecedented. As one of the elders of a formal church said, "I cannot do with the hymns. They are all the time in my head, and I cannot get them out. The psalms never trouble me that way."[16]

The expression "singing the gospel" was first used in England by Rev. A. A. Rees of Sunderland in describing Sankey's soul-stirring hymns. Before Moody and Sankey's campaigns in the British Isles, the title of "Singing Evangelist" had never been used nor had an evangelist been associated with a person to take charge of the music.[17] George Stebbins honored Sankey when he said:

> He brought the service of song in evangelistic movements to the front in so striking a manner, demonstrating its importance as an aid in enforcing the claims of the Gospel upon the world . . . and establishing the custom of evangelists going two by two, preacher and singer, preaching the Word in sermon and song.[18]

Moody and Sankey were pioneers of a new evangelistic method which combined the efforts of evangelist and singer, a method that has persisted to the present day.

While Moody and Sankey were doing their evangelistic work in Britain, P. P. Bliss (1838-1876), a talented musician and composer, was active in Chicago. His life story is similar to that of many gospel song-writers. As a young boy he loved music, and as a teenager he received his first formal musical instruction at a school taught by J. G. Towner. (Towner was the father of the well-known gospel song writer, D. B. Towner.) During his study at Towner's school, he met William Bradbury and became acquainted with his work. Bliss was quite im-

---

14. Robert M. Stevenson, *Patterns of Protestant Church Music,* p. 156.

15. Marvin McKissick, "The Function of Music in American Revivals Since 1875," *The Hymn,* 9 (October, 1958): p. 111.

16. W. H. Daniels, *Moody: His Words, Work, and Workers,* p. 487.

17. P. P. Bliss must be given credit for introducing solos in evangelistic meetings.

18. Stebbins, pp. 206-7.

pressed with Bradbury's music, and it influenced his own musical efforts. Upon graduation, Bliss became active in teaching music in schools and conventions. He later moved to Chicago where he became associated with Root and Cady, a well-known music publishing firm, for whom he wrote many songs. Bliss also traveled for the company, representing it at music conventions.

Bliss first met Moody during the summer of 1869 and began singing in Moody's services between his other engagements. Between this time and 1874, Bliss was the director of music for the First Congregational Church and also its Sunday school superintendent. In the early 1870s, he began writing Sunday school songs. *The Chorus* (Cincinnati, 1871) was his first book published, followed by *Sunshine* in 1873. When reports reached America about the success of Moody and Sankey in England, he turned from writing children's Sunday school songs to composing hymns more suitable for evangelistic work.

While in Scotland, Moody wrote Bliss and the well-known evangelist Major D. W. Whittle and urged them to unite their efforts. After a successful meeting together in Waukegen, Illinois, in 1874, they decided to take Moody's advice. During this same year, the John Church Company of Cincinnati published a small collection of *Gospel Hymns* for use in their meetings.[19] It contained fifty-two tunes of Bliss' own composition, many of which were set to words written by him. Louis Benson states:

> The hymns were striking and sometimes dramatic: the tunes were hardly original, being full of old and familiar ideas and phrases, but were of a vivacious sort sure to become popular when they found their opportunity.[20]

This opportunity soon came, when Moody and Sankey returned to America in 1875. Sankey combined his *Sacred Songs and Solos* with Bliss' *Gospel Hymns,* and they were jointly published as *Gospel Hymns and Sacred Songs—By P. P. Bliss and Ira D. Sankey, as used by them in gospel meetings* (Biglow and Main and John Church and Co., 1875). This was the first in a series of five hymnbooks which followed: *Gospel Hymns No. 2* in 1876, *No. 3* in 1878, *No. 4* in 1883, *No. 5* in 1887, and *No. 6* in 1891. These books became extremely popular; their co-publication added greatly to their circulation and distribution. It is said that over fifty million were sold.[21] The series culminated in *Gospel Hymns Nos. 1-6 Complete* (1894), which contained 739 hymns. After

19. Sankey is usually credited with originating the term "gospel hymn."

20. Benson, p. 486.

Sankey's death, an English publisher (Marshall, Morgan and Scott) enlarged the 1891 edition and published it under the title *Sacred Songs and Solos:* "1200 Pieces."

From the time of the first edition of *Gospel Hymns and Sacred Songs* (1875), Bliss became associated with Moody and Sankey in their revival meetings. The hymnbook was introduced in their first major meeting in America, which was held in Brooklyn Rink in New York City. Henry Wilder Foote attributed the long-continued success of the Moody revival meetings to the vogue of *Gospel Hymns and Sacred Songs.*[22] The success of this hymnbook was unprecedented; only the English Bible outsold it at the time.[23] The hymns it contained united thousands of unchurched people with a common song. Of these hymns Louis Benson says, "The new melodies penetrated even the music halls and were whistled by the man on the street."[24] Many of the hymns became "household songs," especially, "Ho, My Comrades, See the Signal," "Let the Lower Lights Be Burning," and "Almost Persuaded Now to Believe" by Bliss; "Safe in the Arms of Jesus" and "Rescue the Perishing" by Fanny Crosby; "The Ninety and Nine" and "A Shelter in the Time of Storm" by Sankey.

Sankey's singing of gospel hymns played an important part in Moody's ministry. Other than preaching the Bible itself, Sankey's and Bliss' gospel hymns were the main medium for reaching people for Christ. Upon Bliss' tragic death in a train accident, Moody wrote:

I believe he was raised up of God to write hymns for the Church of Christ in this age, as Charles Wesley was for the Church in his day. His songs have gone around the world, and have led, and will continue to lead, hundreds of souls to Christ. In my estimate he was the most highly honored of God of any man of his time, as a writer and singer of Gospel songs; and, with all his gifts, he was the most humble man I ever knew.[25]

The effectiveness of Sankey's singing of hymns found in *Gospel Hymns and Sacred Solos* is illustrated in this account of one of the services at the Brooklyn Rink:

---

21. Charles E. Gold, "The Gospel Song: Contemporary Opinion," *The Hymn*, 9 (July, 1958), p. 69.

22. Foote, p. 266.

23. R. A. Lapsley, *The Songs of Zion*, p. 20.

24. Benson, p. 487.

25. Carey Bonner, *Some Baptist Hymnists*, p. 123-4.

Mr. Moody had said, immediately after reading from the Bible, "I am going to ask Mr. Sankey to sing the 120th Hymn alone"—a sharp emphasis on the last word. The instant hush of expectation as the great audience[26] settled back prepared to hear something that should appeal to their hearts, was very marked, but as Mr. Sankey's magnetic voice and wonderfully expressive singing filled the great auditorium, the sympathy among his hearers grew and increased until it seemed as if, had he continued the sweet melody and earnest supplication, every person in the whole audience would have risen and joined with him in a grand musical prayer of mingled appeal and thanksgiving. The effect he produced was simply marvelous. Many responses, such as "amen" and "Glory to God," were heard from all parts of the vast assembly, and at the close a great many men as well as women were in tears.[27]

Thus, the gospel song appeared as an answer to a specific need, a need that has always accompanied spiritual revivals. That need was for a popular religious song which would reach people with the personal message of salvation. Erik Routley expanded the area of the individual's spiritual need when he confessed:

Some of us have poked fun at the tribe jingles of the Sankey revival. But trapped miners have sung, "Hold the Fort," and who knows how many people have calmed elemental fears of death with "Shall We Gather At the River?" and beaten off the growing fear of hunger and insecurity and dispossession with, "Will Your Anchor Hold?"[28]

The gospel hymns of Sankey, Bliss, and others provided an emotional outlet for the individual and also fulfilled his need to express his personal testimony.

Bliss and Sankey became the leaders of an evangelistic school of music which has lasted to the present day. This is not to say that the movement of popular religious song was initiated by them, but rather that under their direction an older movement reached its apex and came to great success.

This success was certainly distinctive and introduced the modern era of revival song. But new hymn writers and composers emerged on the scene to continue the tradition of the gospel song. Among these new

---

26. Moody and Sankey always drew large crowds: 5,000 each night in Brooklyn and at their next meeting in Philadelphia, 13,000. The crowds included people from every walk of life, drunkards, cultured atheists, prominent citizens, church members; young and old, musical and non-musical. James Sydnor, *The Hymn and Congregational Singing* (Richmond: John Knox, 1960), p. 66.

27. E. J. Goodspeed, *A Full History of the Wonderful Career of Moody and Sankey, In Great Britain and America*, p. 230.

28. Erik Routley, *Hymns and Human Life*, p. 152.

hymnists, such names as James McGranahan ("There Shall Be Showers of Blessing"), George C. Stebbins ("Saved by Grace"), Charles C. Converse ("What a Friend We Have in Jesus"), Charles Gabriel ("Since Jesus Came into My Heart"), and George Bennard ("The Old Rugged Cross") are perhaps the best known.

Charles Alexander

The emphasis on presenting the gospel message in song was continued after Moody and Sankey by several other evangelistic teams. The first noteworthy team included a Moody Bible Institute graduate, Charles Alexander (1867-1920), the song leader for evangelist R. A. Torrey. Alexander was also the song leader for another well-known evangelist of that time, J. Wilbur Chapman. These men altered Moody's mode of mass evangelism by working more within the framework of the local church.

Charles Alexander's three most important contributions to evangelistic music were (1) the substitution of piano accompaniment for the organ, (2) the combination of the song leader's responsibilities with those of a master of ceremonies, and (3) the introduction of the "chorus"[29] into congregational singing.

The use of the piano in the song service tended to enliven the singing,[30] and it called for the composition of gospel songs with an even greater rhythmic drive. Alexander's method of "warming up" the audience drew them in as more active participants in the service. Because of the urbanization and increased sophistication of American society, audience response had greatly decreased compared to the days of the camp meeting. Alexander's approach—to unify the people through singing—was welcomed by the city-dwellers who felt lost and insecure in the complexities of urban life. His use of the chorus to inspire enthusiastic singing is still popular today, especially in fundamental churches where there is a demand for a more inspirational type of service. Musically, Alexander prepared the way for Homer Rodeheaver, the music director for Billy Sunday.

---

29. The form of the "chorus" is generally one stanza in length and set to an easily sung melody. Many times the ryhthm is quite energetic. The subject matter is varied, but usually the text expresses the joy of living for Jesus or the anticipation of His second coming. Some choruses are similar to the camp meeting chorus with frequent repetition of words.

30. A description of the practice of improvising accompaniments to gospel hymns is given in James C. Downey, "The Gospel Hymn 1875-1930" (M.A. thesis, University of Southern Mississippi, 1963), pp. 130-40.

The Billy Sunday Campaigns

Billy Sunday followed the precedent set by Sankey and teamed up with a song leader, Homer A. Rodeheaver, in 1910. Building upon Alexander's song-leading techniques, Rodeheaver continued the tradition of making the enthusiastic singing of gospel songs almost entirely dependent upon the ability of the song leader to inspire the congregation. (Today, when someone refers to a particular congregation as one that "really sings," the usual question in response is, "Who leads it?") Rodeheaver had the ability to draw a crowd into the service by sensing its mood and responding appropriately with his musical ability and sense of humor.

The songs composed and used by Rodeheaver were doctrinally similar to Sankey's, but the song services in the Billy Sunday meetings were more enthusiastic and light-hearted. Moody seldom used songs with a self-confident tone like "Onward, Christian Soldiers"; Sunday liked the triumphant tone of "The Battle Hymn of the Republic" and "Onward, Christian Soldiers." In fact, Rodeheaver's hymnbook contained a whole section of songs devoted to warfare.

Another characteristic of Sunday's meetings was the large choir. Sankey's choirs of two or three hundred singers were small compared to Rodeheaver's choirs, which sometimes boasted as many as two thousand voices. William T. Ellis, one of Sunday's biographers, has said:

> The tabernacle music in itself is enough to draw the great throngs which nightly crowd the building. The choir furnished not only the melodies but also a rare spectacle. . . . Without his choir Sunday could scarcely conduct his great campaigns.[31]

In Moody's meetings, the main purpose of the choir was to help direct the congregational singing, but in Sunday's meetings the choir was an integral part of the music portion of the service. Occasionally, the choir would sing pieces such as the "Hallelujah Chorus," "Unfold, Ye Portals," or the "Gloria" from Mozart's *Twelfth Mass;* however, most of their numbers were selections of the old hymns and newer gospel songs.[32] Rodeheaver bore witness to the value of Charles Gabriel's songs when he said:

> Without "Brighten the Corner," "Sail On," "My Wonderful Dream," and "Awakening Chorus"—not to mention others—I could not have held the immense choirs and tremendous audiences I have had to quiet and control.[33]

---

31. William T. Ellis, *Billy Sunday, The Man and His Message,* p. 263.

32. McKissick, p. 113.   33. Stebbins, p. 325.

Sunday and Rodeheaver, like those who preceded them, were successful in presenting the gospel through fiery preaching, and through the personal warmth of the gospel song. Describing the purpose of the gospel song, Rodeheaver said:

> The gospel song is a declaration of God's plan of salvation and his promises, addressed to the people. We can bring you thousands of illustrations of individuals whose lives have actually been changed by the message of the gospel song, and who have become assets in their communities where they were liabilities before. These songs are not written for prayer meetings, but to challenge the attention of people on the outside who have not been interested in any form of church work or worship. They are used simply as a step from nothing to something. If critics knew how some of these songs were loved by many people, they would never refer to the 'saccharine talents' of great and good men who have blessed the world with their songs.[34]

Rodeheaver continued to compose gospel songs and lead people in the singing of them until his death in 1955.

The Billy Graham Evangelistic Team

A new age of mass evangelism was introduced by Billy Graham and his evangelistic team, which first began its world-wide crusade ministry in 1954. Graham could have made the same observation made by Erik Routley:

> We stand now, therefore at the opening of a new age. . . . Our judgment of the Sankey songs, and hymns of that kind, must rest on the ground that they were designed for a special purpose, whether we continue to use them depends on whether we think they are the best instruments for achieving the same purpose today.[35]

Graham's main purpose appears to be no different from that of all other evangelists since Wesley and Whitefield—that of winning the lost to Jesus. No doubt Graham observed, like those who preceded him, that God is not restricted by simple words or by what many regard as inferior music; the Spirit of God does indeed seem to put His approval on simple, gospel lyrics as "a favored instrumentality for salvation of immortal souls."[36] And so Graham continued to use the gospel song, directed by song leader Cliff Barrows. Melton Wright once said as he

---

34. Howard, p. 366.

35. Routley, p. 240.

36. Lapsley, p. 22.

observed Barrows in action: "You're convinced that Barrows' specialty is making singing irresistible to multitudes."[37] Barrows usually uses one standard hymn for congregational singing in a service, and the remainder of the song service consists of gospel songs. Perhaps the two most popular gospel songs at Graham's "crusades" are Fanny Crosby's "Blessed Assurance" and Carl Boberg's "How Great Thou Art."

Other than Barrows' dynamic leadership, the musical success of the Graham crusades can be attributed to the massive choirs and gospel soloists—George Beverly Shea in particular. The crusade choirs are usually many times larger even than the chorus which sang in the Billy Sunday meetings. Very little new music is used; the choir "specials" are usually standard hymn and gospel song arrangements. As we noted, some of Moody's success depended upon Sankey's vocal ability and his rapport with the audience; so it is with George Beverly Shea and the Graham crusades. As Marvin McKissick explains, "When Shea steps to the pulpit, and with deep reverence begins to sing, 'I'd rather have Jesus than silver or gold,' you understand in a small measure the reason for the success of the team."[38]

Jack and Rexella Van Impe

Jack Van Impe, a contemporary of Billy Graham, is also at the forefront of twentieth-century revivalism. The city-wide crusades held by the Van Impe Team have become especially prominent since 1970. Van Impe has maintained the continuity of the revivalist's message of repentance of sin and faith in Jesus Christ for salvation. However, he emphasizes Bible prophecy and America's relationship to "end-time" events more than the evangelists of the past. His methods of mass evangelism are similar to those who have preceded him. Van Impe's city-wide crusades, held in large auditoriums and stadiums, utilize large choirs (comparable in size to those at Moody's meetings). Van Impe has published special crusade choir books which, for the most part, contain traditional gospel song arrangements. During the crusades, the choirs are usually led by guest conductors from fundamental churches in the area.

The two striking differences between the Van Impe team and all preceeding revivalists are that he is an accomplished musician, and that the other member of his team is his wife, Rexella. Mrs. Van Impe, a concert pianist and a talented vocalist, accompanies the congregational

---

37. Melton Wright, "How Cliff Barrows Does It," *Christian Herald,* (November 1955), p. 25.

38. McKissick, p. 115.

singing and provides most of the "special" music. Her repertoire consists of traditional and contemporary gospel songs sung to taped orchestral accompaniments. Van Impe impresses crowds with his artistry on the accorgan. He usually plays one or more concert pieces during a crusade, and at every service he plays several gospel song arrangements. "Dwelling in Beulah Land" is, perhaps, the one played most frequently.

Congregational singing remains an important part of the services. Song sheets, distributed each evening, contain the lyrics of nineteen gospel songs such as "Jesus Saves," "Amazing Grace," "Power in the Blood," "He Lives," and "Revive Us Again."

Jack Van Impe and Billy Graham bring to a close one hundred years (1875-1975) of mass evangelism in America. As we have noted, the methods and the message of the evangelists are much the same today as they were one hundred years ago. The music also appears to be nearly the same. There has been one notable change, however, in the music: the subject matter. The following table, compiled by Marvin McKissick[39] and myself, is a comparison of the subject matter of the revival songs used in the Moody, Sankey, Graham, and Van Impe revivals. The percentages in each case were obtained by examining the songbooks most used in each of the four revival movements.

	Moody Revivals	Sunday Revivals	Graham Revivals	Van Impe Revivals
Songs of Exhortation and Invitation	35%	20%	35%	26%
Songs of Doctrine and Faith	25%	15%	24%	16%
Songs of Rejoicing	10%	25%	30%	37%
Songs of Death, Judgment, and Heaven	24%	15%	9%	16%
Songs of Sentiment	2%	10%	–	–
Songs dealing with Contemporary Political Issues	1%	5%	–	–
Songs of Warfare	3%	10%	2%	5%

The table indicates certain similarities between the Moody and Graham revivals, especially in the first two categories. Similarities are also noted between the revivals of Sunday and Van Impe in the first

---

39. Ibid.

two and fourth categories. It is clear that there has been a steady increase in the percentage of "songs of rejoicing" and a steady decrease in the use of "songs of death and judgment." (The Van Impe crusades show a marked increase probably because of his emphasis on prophecy.) Overall, the songs of the Moody and Graham revivals are very similar in subject matter, as are those of the Sunday and Van Impe revivals.

The vocal music of modern revivalism has remained essentially the same as revivalism in the past. Each of the four revivalists (Moody, Sunday, Graham, and Van Impe) have used a large choir and one principal soloist. The mass choirs in the Moody and Van Impe revivals were generally smaller than those in the Sunday and Graham revivals, but congregational song remained an important part of all services. The evangelists found it to unify the thought of people and to prepare them for the preaching of the Word. As George Stebbins states:

> The great service of song, as it has been used in evangelistic movements, was without question called forth providentially to be used as a handmaid to the preaching of the Word, as has been attested throughout its history by the seal of God's approval.[40]

Louis Benson said that the Moody and Sankey revivals were able to bring about "a new phase of hymn singing as notable in its day as the eighteenth century Methodist song.[41] Upon observing meetings of Graham and Van Impe, it appears that there has been no decrease in the importance of congregational song since the revivals held by Moody and Sankey some one hundred years ago.

Gospel Songs in the Ministry
Of the Local Church

We have traced the gospel song and its beginnings through the great revival movements since the time of John and Charles Wesley. Popular religious song was, for the most part, contained within revival movements outside the local church. In fact, both advocates and opponents of the gospel song were of the opinion that revival songs did not belong in the ordinary worship service. However, gospel songs have been increasingly used in the church service, and many, if not most, evangelistic churches now use them almost exclusively.

---

40. Stebbins, p. 326.

41. Benson, p. 488.

It is not my purpose to discuss the gospel song's place in the public service, but a few observations are necessary to understand its current development and use.

For hundreds of years, evengelism was considered a secondary function of Christianity; one which should take place outside the ministry of the local church. This was graphically illustrated in the camp meeting and Y.M.C.A. movements of the nineteenth century. There have been notable exceptions, however, to this attitude—R. A. Torrey was one evangelist who worked closely with the local church.

Within the last fifty to seventy-five years, many pastors and evangelists have become convinced that the primary purpose of the church is to evangelize. They point out that Jesus Christ was speaking to the church when He said, "Go ye into all the world, and preach the gospel to every creature" (Mark 16:15). The renewed conviction that the primary ministry of the church is to reach the masses with the gospel has manifested the need for popular religious song within the local church. Thus, thousands of American churches within the past fifty years have added the gospel song to the congregation's repertoire of standard hymns.

The largest portion of gospel songs used in churches today were composed and written by people such as P. P. Bliss, Fanny Crosby, B. B. McKinney, E. O. Excell, Charles Gabriel, and D. E. Towner. Several contemporary composers and writers have produced songs that are fast becoming standards in many gospel song collections. Perhaps the most notable composer is John W. Peterson, who has done most of his work in composing cantatas. (These range in subject matter from the Christmas and Easter stories to cantatas with missionary emphases.) He has also written hundreds of gospel songs for soloists and small ensembles and compiled them in many collections. Relying on the traditional idiom, Peterson has also composed many gospel songs which are used in congregational singing. Among the more popular are "Heaven Came Down," "So Send I You," and "Jesus Is Coming Again."

Other current gospel song composers whose songs are adaptable to congregational singing are John R. Rice, Ira F. Stanphill, Oswald J. Smith, and Alfred Smith. Alfred Smith is, perhaps, the most prolific composer after Peterson.

Conclusion

Lyman Abbot, in the introduction to *The Plymouth Hymnal* (New York, 1894), said of the "Gospel Hymn" school:

> Music has become the expression of the spiritual life for thousands who before were without a voice in public worship, and, as suppressed feeling easily dies, were often without any share in public worship.[1]

Abbot's opinion that "feeling easily dies" if there is no congregational song available to express one's personal spiritual experiences could just as easily have been voiced by Isaac Watts, John and Charles Wesley, and all others prominent in the history of popular religious song.

Two elements of congregational song have been traced in this survey: subjective lyrics and popular melodies. These elements, merged into a unified whole, characterize the gospel song. The simple, straightforward music developed from these two elements has always been (and, in my opinion, will be for some time to come) closely related to the evangelistic goals of fundamental churches and revival movements.

It must be remembered that Christ often used the common things of life to reach the multitude. And so, the gospel song must be judged on its own merits and not compared to the standard hymn. Each, of course, has its place and purpose. Most important, the goals of any religious body will determine the type of song it will utilize. The gospel

---

1. Benson, p. 489.

song is significant because it is related to a primary goal of the church, that of reaching people for Christ. The gospel song and its antecedents have been used successfully by the church and the revival movements to reach this goal.

The gospel song began as a protest against the staid music of organized religious sects and has been developed over a four-hundred-year period by a devoutly Christian people. What began as a protest has become a means of insight into the needs of twentieth-century man. And his need, regardless of his sophistication, is for a right relationship with God. This idea is expressed in all gospel songs; songs that can be grasped by all the people.

Appendix

Musical and Textual Analysis
Of the Gospel Song

As we attempt to define the term "gospel song," and differentiate it from the term "hymn," we find that there is no agreement among authorities about what constitutes a "hymn" or a "gospel song." For the purpose of this discussion, the following definitions have been chosen.

> *Hymn.* A Christian hymn is a lyric poem, reverently and devotionally conceived, which is designed to be sung and which expresses the worshiper's attitude toward God, or God's purposes in human life. It is simple and metrical in form, genuinely emotional, poetic and literary in style, spiritual in quality, and in its ideas so direct and so immediately apparent as to unify a congregation while singing it.[1]

> *Gospel song.* The term "gospel song" is applied to a certain class of sacred lyrics, chiefly of an evangelistic character, composed for use in popular gatherings of a heterogeneous character.[2]

The words of the gospel songs

> . . . are usually simple and easily remembered and concern themselves largely with the individual's salvation. The personal pronouns "I" and "my" predominate. The tunes are rhythmic and catchy and always have a refrain added.[3]

Basically, gospel songs are songs of testimony, persuasion, exhortation, or warning. The chorus or refrain technique is often found in the gospel song.

In order to arrive at a clearer understanding of the nature of the gospel song, we must examine its musical and textual characteristics. Various examples of the gospel song will be surveyed here which indicate essential characteristics of both text and tune. The gospel songs which are included in this study represent such composers as Bliss, Doane, McGranahan, and Bradbury. The majority of the examples used may be found in *Sacred Songs and Solos* (London: Marshall, Morgan & Scott). The selections are categorized to indicate the major characteristics of gospel songs in general, but there is an obvious overlapping in the various categories.

---

1. Carol F. Price, *What Is a Hymn,* Paper Number VI. The official definition of the Hymn Society of America, p. 8.

2. Breed, p. 331.

3. Lester Hostetler, *Handbook to the Mennonite Hymnary,* pp. xxvii-xxviii.

Musical example of a Sunday school song.

Growing Brighter

Words and Music by
G. T. WILSON

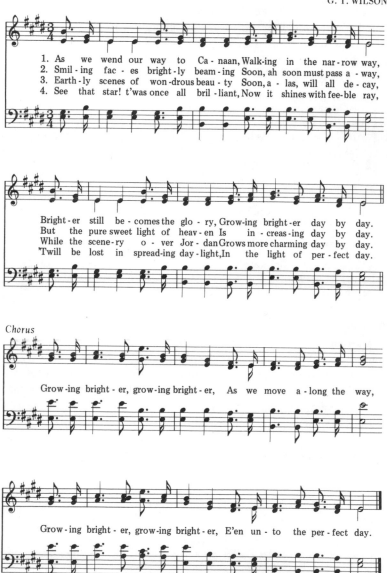

Figure 1

Figures 2, 3. An evangelistic fervor and concern for the lost and dying are illustrated in these examples. The music contains the familiar verse and chorus technique typical of so many gospel songs.

Throw Out the Life-Line

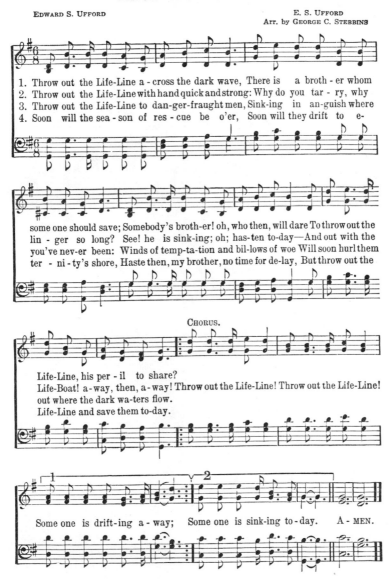

Figure 2

Let the Lower Lights Be Burning

Figure 3

Figures 4, 5, 6. In these three examples, the tenor and bass part echo the soprano and alto, a characteristic of some gospel songs. The harmony used in these pieces is quite simple, consisting predominately of the tonic, dominant, and subdominant chords. One use of a secondary dominant is found in the penultimate measure of Figure 4.

Christ Receiveth Sinful Men

Figure 4

Figure 5

Sweet By and By

Figure 6

Figures 7, 8, 9. These examples of congregational songs border the categories of hymn and gospel song. Some hymnologists have noted that there is no absolute line of demarcation between the two categories. Although none of these examples contain a chorus, their intrinsic character is very close to that of the gospel song.

There Is a Fountain

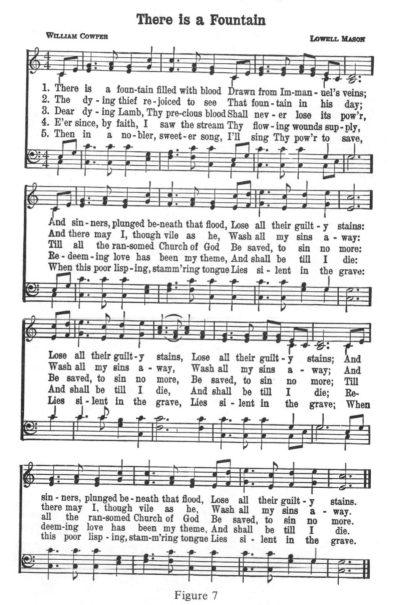

Figure 7

Stand Up for Jesus

Figure 8

My Jesus, I Love Thee

Author Unknown

A. J. GORDON

1. My Je - sus, I love Thee, I know Thou art mine, For Thee all the fol - lies of sin I re - sign; My gra - cious Re - deem - er, my Sav - ior art Thou; If ev - er I loved Thee, my Je - sus, 'tis now.

2. I love Thee, be - cause Thou hast first lov - ed me, And pur-chased my par - don on Cal - va - ry's tree; I love Thee for wear - ing the thorns on Thy brow: If ev - er I loved Thee, my Je - sus, 'tis now.

3. I'll love Thee in life, I will love Thee in death, And praise Thee as long as Thou lend - est me breath; And say when the death - dew lies cold on my brow, If ev - er I loved Thee, my Je - sus, 'tis now.

4. In man - sions of glo - ry and end - less de - light, I'll ev - er a- dore Thee in heav - en so bright; I'll sing with the glit - ter - ing crown on my brow, If ev - er I loved Thee, my Je - sus, 'tis now.

Figure 9

Figures 10, 11, 12. The texts of these songs emphasize accepting Christ as Lord and Savior. They are songs of persuasion, pleading, and warning, and are used during "altar calls" and consecration services.

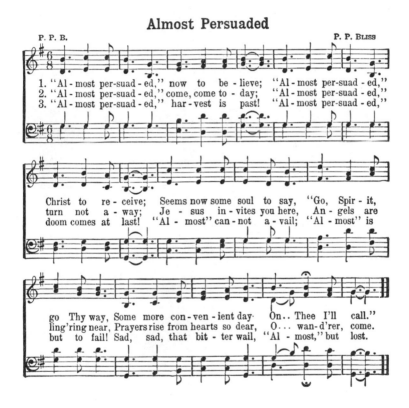

Figure 10

Figure 11

Just As I Am

CHARLOTTE ELLIOTT

WILLIAM B. BRADBURY

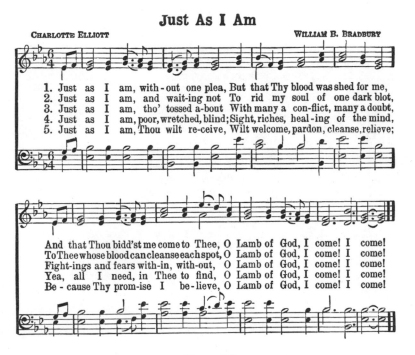

1. Just as I am, with-out one plea, But that Thy blood was shed for me,
2. Just as I am, and wait-ing not To rid my soul of one dark blot,
3. Just as I am, tho' tossed a-bout With many a con-flict, many a doubt,
4. Just as I am, poor, wretched, blind; Sight, riches, heal-ing of the mind,
5. Just as I am, Thou wilt re-ceive, Wilt welcome, pardon, cleanse, relieve;

And that Thou bidd'st me come to Thee, O Lamb of God, I come! I come!
To Thee whose blood can cleanse each spot, O Lamb of God, I come! I come!
Fight-ings and fears with-in, with-out, O Lamb of God, I come! I come!
Yea, all I need, in Thee to find, O Lamb of God, I come! I come!
Be - cause Thy prom-ise I be-lieve, O Lamb of God, I come! I come!

Figure 12

Figures 13, 14, 15. These are illustrative of the gospel song emphasis upon Heaven and the future life.

Figure 13

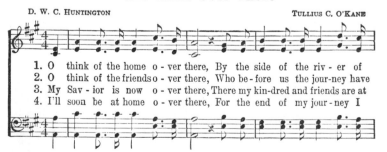

Figure 14

Beulah Land

Figure 15

Figures 16, 17, 18. These gospel songs are songs of personal testimony. The texts contain many references to the singer's own emotions and experiences ("my life," "my heart," "my longings," "my story"). This personal point of view is typical of gospel songs.

Figure 16

Figure 17

Blessed Assurance

Figure 18

Comparison of Hymn and Gospel Song

These gospel songs have been selected in an attempt to help formulate a definition of the gospel song. The texts and the music of the examples possess characteristics and structure of the majority of gospel songs.

In his attempt to distinguish between the hymn and the gospel song, Charles Gold drew up the following table:[4]

THE HYMN	THE GOSPEL SONG
1. Primary purpose is to glorify God. Both objective and subjective in character.	1. Primarily a song of exhortation, testimony, warning, persuasion. Usually subjective in character.
2. Used primarily in worship services.	2. Used primarily in revival meetings, evangelistic services, and fellowship periods.
3. Music is stately, dignified, and devotional in character.	3. Usually rhythmically fast. A pervasive enthusiasm.
4. Notes of even time value. Comparatively few notes of eighth or sixteenth value.	4. Notes of varied time value, containing, at times, dotted eighths and sixteenths.
5. Text is usually set to music without use of chorus or refrain technique.	5. Verse with chorus or refrain pattern predominating.

4. Charles E. Gold, *A Study of The Gospel Song* (Unpublished Thesis, University of Southern California, 1953), pp. 88-89.

The Text

When analyzing the text of the gospel song, Paul Dear compared the subject matter of the nineteenth- and twentieth-century hymn with that of the gospel song. The following chart is based on his study:[5]

HYMNS	GOSPEL SONGS
1. Pertain to earthly life of Jesus.	1. Pertain to present and future work of Christ.
2. Few references to the older and traditional interpretations of the church.	2. Many references to the older and traditional interpretations of the church.
3. Many are concerned with Christ's present task as one which concerns social issues.	3. Christ's present task is general in scope rather than one limited to particular issues. He is pictured as One at work in the world seeking to save the souls of men.
4. Comparatively few show an interest in the Second Coming of Christ.	4. An interest in the Second Coming of Christ.
5. An emphasis on the moral influence of the cross.	5. More reference to the death of Jesus on the Cross and to His resurrection.
6. A preference of referring to the humanity of Jesus.	6. A preference of referring to the divinity of Jesus.
7. Names and titles given to Christ reflect Jesus' humanity and relation to man such as "Son of Man," "Our Elder Brother," "Master."	7. Names and titles given to Christ reflect the redemptive work of Christ such as "Lamb of God," "Redeemer," "Savior."

The Christological interpretation in the texts of gospel songs has been the consistent interpretation of evangelical hymn writers from the time of Watts to present day writers.

In another examination of gospel song texts, Waldemar Hille states:

It has much in common with the subjective hymns, as for the most part, it is primarily concerned with personal salvation or exhortation. . . . The words of some Gospel songs are rather vivid pictorial representations like "Life is like a mountain railroad," and the thoughts are expressed simply and directly. This is responsible for the way so many Gospel songs catch the popular imagination.[6]

---

5. Paul Dear, *Christology As Expressed in Protestant Hymns* (Unpublished Thesis, The University of Southern California, 1941).

6. Waldemar Hille, "Evaluating Gospel Songs," *The Hymn,* 3 (January 1951): p. 17.

The Music

Compared to the music of standard hymns, the music of gospel songs is relatively simple. The harmony is usually based upon the tonic, dominant, and subdominant chords, with occasional use of a secondary dominant. There are few changes in harmony, usually one chord change per measure and sometimes only one chord change per phrase. Seldom is there modulation, and when present, it is only temporarily to the nearest related key. The rhythm is usually strongly defined: a march tempo, waltz tempo, or contemplative. Many gospel songs employ dotted rhythms such as dotted eighth-sixteenth.

The form of the music is usually that of a double period. The musical scheme is most often either ABA or AB. The tunes are usually written in a major mode and are easy to learn and remember. Gospel songs, though generally sung in unison, are written in four-part harmony. Figures 4, 5, and 6 illustrate imitation by the male voices which echo the melody sung by the female voices.

Lester Hostetler said in his *Handbook to the Mennonite Hymnary* that "The masses of the people readily learned to sing these tunes and experienced a thrill in singing them which the use of the more stately and solid hymns failed to effect."[7] Many gospel songs are so successful and popular because they have a wide appeal and can be sung by everybody.

---

7. Hostetler, p. xxvii.

Bibliography

Books

Allen, Cecil J. *Hymns and the Christian Faith.* London: Pickering & Inglis Ltd., 1966.

Appleby, David P. *History of Church Music.* Chicago: Moody Press, 1965.

Benson, Louis F. *The English Hymn.* New York: George H. Doran Company, 1915; reprint ed., Richmond, Virginia: John Knox Press, 1962.

Bonner, Carey. *Some Baptist Hymnists.* London: Kingsgate Press, 1937.

Brawley, Benjamin. *History of the English Hymn.* New York: The Abingdon Press, 1932.

Breed, David R. *The History and Use of Hymns and Hymn-Tunes.* New York: Fleming H. Revell Company, 1903.

Chase, Gilbert. *America's Music.* 2d ed. New York: McGraw-Hill Book Company, 1966.

Daniels, W. H. *Moody: His Words, Work, and Workers.* New York: Nelson and Phillips, 1877.

Dearnley, Christopher. *English Church Music 1650-1750 In Royal Chapel, Cathedral and Parish Church.* Erik Routley Series in Church Music. London: Oxford University Press, 1970.

Ellinwood, Leonard. *The History of American Church Music.* New York: Morehouse-Gorham Company, 1953.

Ellis, William T. *Billy Sunday, The Man and His Message.* Philadelphia: John C. Winston Company, 1914.

Foote, Henry Wilder. *Three Centuries of American Hymnody.* Cambridge: Harvard University Press, 1940.

Frost, Maurice, ed. *Historical Companion to Hymns Ancient and Modern.* London: William Clowes & Sons, Limited, 1962.

Goodspeed, E. J. *A Full History of the Wonderful Career of Moody and Sankey.* New York: Henry S. Goodspeed and Company, 1876; reprint ed., New York: AMS Press, 1973.

Hall, J. H. *Biography of Gospel Song and Hymn Writers.* Chicago: Fleming H. Revell Company, 1914; reprint ed., New York: AMS Press, 1971.

Hitchcock, H. Wiley. *Music in the United States: A Historical Introduction.* Englewood Cliffs, New Jersey: Prentice-Hall, Incorporated, 1969.

Hooper, William Loyd. *Church Music in Transition.* Nashville: Broadman Press, 1963.

Horn, Dorothy D. *Sing to Me of Heaven.* Gainsville, Florida: University of Florida Press, 1970.

Hostetler, Lester. *Handbook to the Mennonite Hymnary.* Newton, Kansas: General Conference of the Mennonite Church of North America; Board of Publications, 1949.

Howard, John Tasker. *Our American Music.* 4th ed. New York: Thomas Y. Crowell Company, 1965.

Jackson, George Pullen. *Spiritual Folk Songs of Early America.* 2d ed. New York: J. J. Augustine Publishers, 1953.

_____. *White Spirituals in the Southern Uplands.* Durham, North Carolina: University of North Carolina Press, 1933; reprint ed., New York: Dover Publications, Incorporated, 1965.

Lapsley, R. A. *The Songs of Zion.* Richmond, Virginia: Presbyterian Committee of Publications, 1925.

Lowens, Irving. *Music and Musicians in Early America.* New York: W. W. Norton & Company, 1964.

McCutchan, Robert G. *Hymns in the Lives of Men.* New York: Abingdon-Cokesbury Press, 1943.

Metcalf, Frank J. *American Writers and Compilers of Sacred Music.* New York: The Abingdon Press, 1925.

Phillips, C. S. *Hymnody Past and Present.* New York: The Macmillan Company, 1937.

Routley, Erik. *Hymns and Human Life.* 2d ed. Grand Rapids: William B. Eerdmans Publishing Company, 1959.

Sankey, Ira D. *My Life and Story of the Gospel Hymns.* New York: Harper & Brothers, 1907.

Sanville, George W. *Forty Gospel Hymn Stories.* Winona Lake, Indiana: The Rodeheaver-Hall Mack Company, 1944.

Sablosky, Irving L. *American Music.* Daniel J. Boonstein Series in the Chicago History of American Civilization. Chicago: The University of Chicago Press, 1969.

Stebbins, George C. *Reminiscences and Gospel Hymn Stories.* New York: George H. Doran Company, 1924; reprint ed., New York: AMS Press, 1971.

Stevenson, Robert M. *Patterns of Protestant Church Music.* Durham, North Carolina: Duke University Press, 1953.

Sydnor, James R. *The Hymn and Congregational Singing.* Richmond, Virginia: John Knox Press, 1960.

Whitley, W. T. *Congregational Hymn-Singing.* London: J. M. Dent & Sons Limited, 1933.

Periodicals

Atkins, Charles L. "The Hymns of Stephen Collins Foster." *The Hymn,* 12 (April 1961): pp. 52-55.

Downey, James C. "Revivalism, The Gospel Songs and Social Reforms." *Journal of The Society For Ethnomusicology,* 9 (May 1965): pp. 115-120.

Gold, Charles E. "The Gospel Song: Contemporary Opinion." *The Hymn,* 9 (July 1958): pp. 69-73.

Hille, Waldemar. "Evaluating Gospel Songs." *The Hymn,* 3 (January 1951): p. 17.

Lowens, Irving. "Our Neglected Musical Heritage." *The Hymn,* 3 April 1952): pp. 51-54.

Lovelace, Austin C. "Early Sacred Folk Music in America." *The Hymn,* 3 (January 1952).

McKissick, Marvin. "The Function of Music in American Revivals Since 1875." *The Hymn,* 9 (October 1958): pp. 107-117.

Papers of the Hymn Society: Number VI, "What Is A Hymn" by Carl F. Price.

Westerman, W. Scott: "The Term 'Gospel Hymn.'" *The Hymn,* 9 (April 1958): pp. 61-62.

Wright, Melton. "How Cliff Barrows Does It." *Christian Herald* (November 1955): p. 25.

Sablosky, Irving L. *American Music.* Daniel J. Boonstein Series in the Chicago History of American Civilization. Chicago: The University of Chicago Press, 1969.

Stebbins, George C. *Reminiscences and Gospel Hymn Stories.* New York: George H. Doran Company, 1924; reprint ed., New York: AMS Press, 1971.

Stevenson, Robert M. *Patterns of Protestant Church Music.* Durham, North Carolina: Duke University Press, 1953.

Sydnor, James R. *The Hymn and Congregational Singing.* Richmond, Virginia: John Knox Press, 1960.

Whitley, W. T. *Congregational Hymn-Singing.* London: J. M. Dent & Sons Limited, 1933.

Periodicals

Atkins, Charles L. "The Hymns of Stephen Collins Foster." *The Hymn,* 12 (April 1961): pp. 52-55.

Downey, James C. "Revivalism, The Gospel Songs and Social Reforms." *Journal of The Society For Ethnomusicology,* 9 (May 1965): pp. 115-120.

Gold, Charles E. "The Gospel Song: Contemporary Opinion." *The Hymn,* 9 (July 1958): pp. 69-73.

Hille, Waldemar. "Evaluating Gospel Songs." *The Hymn,* 3 (January 1951): p. 17.

Lowens, Irving. "Our Neglected Musical Heritage." *The Hymn,* 3 April 1952): pp. 51-54.

Lovelace, Austin C. "Early Sacred Folk Music in America." *The Hymn,* 3 (January 1952).

McKissick, Marvin. "The Function of Music in American Revivals Since 1875." *The Hymn,* 9 (October 1958): pp. 107-117.

Papers of the Hymn Society: Number VI, "What Is A Hymn" by Carl F. Price.

Westerman, W. Scott: "The Term 'Gospel Hymn.' " *The Hymn,* 9 (April 1958): pp. 61-62.

Wright, Melton. "How Cliff Barrows Does It." *Christian Herald* (November 1955): p. 25.

Hymnals

King, E. J. and White, B. F. *The Sacred Harp.* Philadelphia: S. C. Collins Publishing Company, 1859; reprint ed., Nashville: Broadman Press, 1968.

Rice, John R. and Martin, Joy Rice. eds. *Soul-Stirring Songs and Hymns.* Murfreesboro, Tennessee: Sword of the Lord Publishers, 1972.

Sankey, Ira D. *Sacred Songs & Solos.* London: Marshall, Morgan & Scott, Limited, n.d.

Shaw, Knowles. *The Golden Gate.* Cincinnati: John Church and Company, 1874.

Smith, Alfred B. ed. *Living Hymns.* Montrose, Pennsylvania: Encore Publications, Incorporated, 1975.

Other

Dear, Paul W. *Christology As Expressed in Protestant Hymnody, 1620-1900.* Unpublished Thesis, University of Southern California, 1946.

Ferm, Vergilius, *Encyclopedia of Religion.* New York: The Philosophical Library, 1945.

Gold, Charles E. *A Study of the Gospel Song.* Unpublished Thesis, University of Southern California, 1953.

DATE DUE			
JUN 7			
S SEP 30 '83			